FOUR PLAYS OF AESCHYLUS

THE SUPPLIANT MAIDENS

THE PERSIANS

THE SEVEN AGAINST THEBES

THE PROMETHEUS BOUND

TRANSLATED INTO ENGLISH VERSE

BY

E.D.A. MORSHEAD, MA.

INTRODUCTION

The surviving dramas of Aeschylus are seven in number, though he is believed to have written nearly a hundred during his life of sixty-nine years, from 525 B.C. to 456 B.C. That he fought at Marathon in 490, and at Salamis in 480 B.C. is a strongly accredited tradition, rendered almost certain by the vivid references to both battles in his play of *The Persians*, which was produced in 472. But his earliest extant play was, probably, not *The Persians* but *The Suppliant Maidens*—a mythical drama, the fame of which has been largely eclipsed by the historic interest of *The Persians*, and is undoubtedly the least known and least regarded of the seven. Its topic—the flight of the daughters of Danaus from Egypt to Argos, in order to escape from a forced bridal with their first-cousins, the sons of Aegyptus—is legendary, and the lyric element predominates in the play as a whole. We must keep ourselves reminded that the ancient Athenian custom of presenting dramas in *Trilogies-* —that is, in three consecutive plays dealing with different stages of one legend—was probably not uniform: it survives, for us, in one instance only, viz. the Orestean Trilogy, comprising the *Agamemnon*, the *Libation-Bearers*, and the *Eumenides*, or *Furies*. This Trilogy is the masterpiece of the Aeschylean Drama: the four remaining plays of the poet, which are translated in this volume, are all fragments of lost Trilogies—that is to say, the plays are complete as *poems*, but in regard to the poet's larger design they are fragments; they once had predecessors, or sequels, of which only a few words, or lines, or short paragraphs, survive. It is not certain, but seems probable, that the earliest of these single completed plays is *The Suppliant Maidens*, and on that supposition it has been placed first in the present volume. The maidens, accompanied by their father Danaes, have fled from Egypt and arrived at Argos, to take sanctuary there and to avoid capture by their pursuing kinsmen and suitors. In the course of the play, the pursuers' ship arrives to reclaim the maidens for a forced wedlock in Egypt. The action of the drama turns on the attitude of the king and people of Argos, in view of this intended abduction. The king puts the question to the popular vote, and the demand of the suitors is unanimously rejected: the play closes with thanks and gratitude on the part of the fugitives, who, in lyrical strains of quiet beauty, seem to refer the whole question of their marriage to the subsequent decision of the gods, and, in particular, of Aphrodite.

Of the second portion of the Trilogy we can only speak conjecturally. There is a passage in the *Prometheus Bound* (ll. 860-69), in which we learn that the maidens were somehow reclaimed by the suitors, and that all, except one, slew their bridegrooms on the wedding night. There is a faint trace, among the Fragments of Aeschylus, of a play called *Thalamopoioi*,—i.e. *The Preparers of the Chamber*,—which may well have referred to this tragic scene. Its grim title will recall to all classical readers the magnificent, though terrible, version of the legend, in the final stanzas of the eleventh poem in the third book of Horace's *Odes*. The final play was probably called *The Danaides*, and described the acquittal of the brides through some intervention of Aphrodite: a fragment of it survives, in which the goddess appears to be pleading her special prerogative. The legends which commit the daughters of Danaus to an eternal penalty in Hades are, apparently, of later origin. Homer is silent on any such penalty; and Pindar, Aeschylus' contemporary, actually describes the once suppliant maidens as honourably enthroned (*Pyth.* ix. 112: *Nem.* x. ll. 1-10). The Tartarean part of the story is, in fact, post-Aeschylean.

The Suppliant Maidens is full of charm, though the text of the part which describes the arrival of the pursuers at Argos is full of uncertainties. It remains a fine, though archaic, poem, with this special claim on our interest, that it is, probably, the earliest extant poetic drama. We see in it the *tendency* to grandiose language, not yet fully developed as in the *Prometheus*: the inclination of youth to simplicity, and even platitude, in religious and general speculation: and yet we recognize, as in the germ, the profound theology of the *Agamemnon*, and a touch of the political vein which appears more fully in the *Furies*. If the precedence in time here ascribed to it is correct, the play is perhaps worth more recognition than it has received from the countrymen of Shakespeare.

The Persians has been placed second in this volume, as the oldest play whose date is certainly known. It was brought out in 472 B.C., eight years after the sea-fight of Salamis which it commemorates, and five years before the *Seven against Thebes* (467 B.C.). It is thought to be the second play of a Trilogy, standing between the *Phineus* and the *Glaucus*. Phineus was a legendary seer, of the Argonautic era— "Tiresias and Phineus, prophets old"—and the play named after him may have contained a prophecy of the great conflict which is actually described in *The Persae*: the plot of the *Glaucus* is unknown. In any case, *The Persians* was produced before the eyes of a generation which had seen the struggles, West against East, at Marathon and

Thermopylae, Salamis and Plataea. It is as though Shakespeare had commemorated, through the lips of a Spanish survivor, in the ears of old councillors of Philip the Second, the dispersal of the Armada.

Against the piteous want of manliness on the part of the returning Xerxes, we may well set the grave and dignified patriotism of Atossa, the Queen-mother of the Persian kingdom; the loyalty, in spite of their bewilderment, of the aged men who form the Chorus; and, above all, the royal phantom of Darius, evoked from the shadowland by the libations of Atossa and by the appealing cries of the Chorus. The latter, indeed, hardly dare to address the kingly ghost: but Atossa bravely narrates to him the catastrophe, of which, in the lower world, Darius has known nothing, though he realizes that disaster, soon or late, is the lot of mortal power. As the tale is unrolled, a spirit of prophecy possesses him, and he foretells the coming slaughter of Plataea; then, with a last royal admonition that the defeated Xerxes shall, on his return, be received with all ceremony and observance, and with a characteristic warning to the aged men, that they must take such pleasures as they may, in their waning years, he returns to the shades. The play ends with the undignified reappearance of Xerxes, and a melancholy procession into the palace of Susa. It was, perhaps, inevitable that this close of the great drama should verge on the farcical, and that the poltroonery of Xerxes should, in a measure, obscure Aeschylus' generous portraiture of Atossa and Darius. But his magnificent picture of the battle of Salamis is unequalled in the poetic annals of naval war. No account of the flight of the Armada, no record of Lepanto or Trafalgar, can be justly set beside it. The Messenger might well, like Prospero, announce a tragedy by one line—

Sit still, and hear the last of our sea-sorrow.

Five years after *The Persians*, in 467 B. C., the play which we call the *Seven against Thebes* was presented at Athens. It bears now a title which Aeschylus can hardly have given to it for, though the scene of the drama overlooks the region where the city of Thebes afterwards came into being, yet, in the play itself, Thebes is *never* mentioned. The scene of action is the Cadmea, or Citadel of Cadmus, and we know that, in Aeschylus' lifetime, that citadel was no longer a mere fastness, but had so grown outwards and enlarged itself that a new name, Thebes, was applied to the collective city. (All this has been made abundantly clear by Dr. Verrall in his Introduction to the *Seven against Thebes*, to which every reader of the play itself will naturally and most profitably refer.) In the time of Aeschylus, Thebes was, of course, a notable city, his great contemporary Pindar was a citizen of it. But the Thebes of Aeschylus' date is one thing, the fortress represented in Aeschylus' play is quite another, and is never, by him, called Thebes. That the play received, and retains, the name, *The Seven against Thebes*, is believed to be due to two lines of Aristophanes in his *Frogs* (406 B.C.), where he describes Aeschylus' play as "the Seven against Thebes, a drama instinct with War, which any one who beheld must have yearned to be a warrior." This is rather an excellent *description* of the play than the title of it, and could not be its Aeschylean name, for the very sufficient reason that Thebes is not mentioned in the play at all. Aeschylus, in fact, was poetizing an earlier legend of the fortress of Cadmus. This being premised, we may adopt, under protest as it were, the Aristophanic name which has accrued to the play. It is the third part of a Trilogy which might have been called, collectively, *The House of Laius*. Sophocles and Euripides give us *their* versions of the legend, which we may epitomize, without, however, affirming that they followed exactly the lines of Aeschylus Trilogy—they, for instance, speak freely of *Thebes*. Laius, King of Thebes, married Iokaste; he was warned by Apollo that if he had any children ruin would befall his house. But a child was born, and, to avoid the threatened catastrophe, without actually killing the child he exposed it on Mount Cithaeron, that it should die. Some herdsmen saved it and gave it over to the care of a neighbouring king and queen, who reared it. Later on, learning that there was a doubt of his parentage, this child, grown now to maturity, left his foster parents and went to Delphi to consult the oracle, and received a mysterious and terrible warning, that he was fated to slay his father and wed his mother. To avoid this horror, he resolved never to approach the home of his supposed parents. Meantime his real father, Laius, on *his* way to consult the god at Delphi, met his unknown son returning from that shrine—a quarrel fell out, and the younger man slew the elder. Followed by his evil destiny, he wandered on, and found the now kingless Thebes in the grasp of the Sphinx monster, over whom he triumphed, and was rewarded by the hand of Iokaste, his own mother! Not till four children—two sons and two daughters—had been born to them, was the secret of the lineage revealed. Iokaste slew herself in horror, and the wretched king tore out his eyes, that he might never again see the children of his awful union. The two sons quarrelled over the succession, then agreed on a compromise; then fell at variance again, and finally slew each other in single combat. These two sons, according to one tradition, were twins: but the more usual view is that the elder was called Eteocles, the younger, Polynices.

To the point at which the internecine enmity between Eteocles and Polynices arose, we have had to follow Sophocles and Euripides, the first two parts of Aeschylus' Trilogy being lost. But the third part, as we have said, survives under the name given to it by Aristophanes, the *Seven against Thebes*: it opens with an exhortation by Eteocles to his Cadmeans that they should "quit them like men" against the onslaught of Polynices and his Argive allies: the Chorus is a bevy of scared Cadmean maidens, to whom the very sound of war and tramp of horsemen are new and terrific. It ends with the news of the death of the two princes, and the lamentations of their two sisters, Antigone and Ismene. The onslaught from without has been repulsed, but the male line of the house of Laius is extinct. The Cadmeans resolve that Eteocles shall be buried in honour, and Polynices flung to the dogs and birds. Against the latter sentence Antigone protests, and defies the decree: the Chorus, as is natural, are divided in their sentiments.

It is interesting to note that, in combination with the *Laius* and the *Oedipus*, this play won the dramatic crown in 467 B.C. On the other hand, so excellent a judge as Mr. Gilbert Murray thinks that it is "perhaps among Aeschylus' plays the one that bears least the stamp of commanding genius." Perhaps the daring, practically atheistic, character of Eteocles; the battle-fever that burns and thrills through the play; the pathetic terror of the Chorus—may have given it favour, in Athenian eyes, as the work of a poet who— though recently (468 B.C.) defeated in the dramatic contest by the young Sophocles—was yet present to tell, not by mere report, the tale of Marathon and Salamis. Or the preceding plays, the *Laius* and the *Oedipus*, may have been of such high merit as to make up for defects observable in the one that still survives. In any case, we can hardly err in accepting Dr. Verral's judgment that "the story of Aeschylus may be, and in the outlines probably is, the genuine epic legend of the Cadmean war."

There remains one Aeschylean play, the most famous—unless we except the *Agamemnon*—in extant Greek literature, the *Prometheus Bound*. That it was the first of a Trilogy, and that the second and third parts were called the *Prometheus Freed*, and *Prometheus the Fire-Bearer*, respectively, is accepted: but the date of its performance is unknown.

The *Prometheus Bound* is conspicuous for its gigantic and strictly superhuman plot. The *Agamemnon* is human, though legendary the *Prometheus* presents to us the gods of Olympus in the days when mankind crept like emmets upon the earth or dwelt in caves, scorned by Zeus and the other powers of heaven, and—still aided by Prometheus the Titan—wholly without art or science, letters or handicrafts. For his benevolence towards oppressed mankind, Prometheus is condemned by Zeus to uncounted ages of pain and torment, shackled and impaled in a lonely cleft of a Scythian precipice. The play opens with this act of divine resentment enforced by the will of Zeus and by the handicraft of Hephaestus, who is aided by two demons, impersonating Strength and Violence. These agents if the ire of Zeus disappear after the first scene, the rest of the play represents Prometheus in the mighty solitude, but visited after a while by a Chorus of sea nymphs who, from the distant depths of ocean, have heard the clang of the demons' hammers, and arrive, in a winged car, from the submarine palace of their father Oceanus. To them Prometheus relates his penalty and its cause: viz., his over tenderness to the luckless race of mankind. Oceanus himself follows on a hippogriff, and counsels Prometheus to submit to Zeus. But the Titan who has handled the sea nymphs with all gentleness, receives the advice with scorn and contempt, and Oceanus retires. But the courage which he lacks his daughters possess to the full; they remain by Prometheus to the end, and share his fate, literally in the crack of doom. But before the end, the strange half human figure of Io, victim of the lust of Zeus and the jealousy of Hera, comes wandering by, and tells Prometheus of her wrongs. He, by his divine power, recounts to her not only the past but also the future of her wanderings. Then, in a fresh access of frenzy, she drifts away into the unknown world. Then Prometheus partly reveals to the sea maidens his secret, and the mysterious cause of Zeus' hatred against him—a cause which would avail to hurl the tyrant from his power. So deadly is this secret, that Zeus will, in the lapse of ages, be forced to reconcile himself with Prometheus, to escape dethronement. Finally, Hermes, the messenger of Zeus, appears with fresh threats, that he may extort the mystery from the Titan. But Prometheus is firm, defying both the tyrant and his envoy, though already the lightning is flashing, the thunder rolling, and sky and sea are mingling their fury. Hermes can say no more; the sea nymphs resolutely refuse to retire, and wait their doom. In this crash of the world, Prometheus flings his final defiance against Zeus, and amid the lightnings and shattered rocks that are overwhelming him and his companions, speaks his last word, "*It is unjust!*"

Any spectacular representation of this finale must, it is clear, have roused intense sympathy with the Titan and the nymphs alike. If, however, the sequel-plays had survived to us, we might conceivably have found and realized another and less intolerable solution. The name *Zeus*, in Greek, like that of *God*, in English, comprises very diverse views of divine personality. The Zeus in the *Prometheus* has little but the name in common with the Zeus in the first chorus of the *Agamemnon*, or in *The Suppliant Maidens* (ll. 86-103): and parallel reflections will give us much food for thought. But, in any case, let us realize that the *Prometheus* is not a human play: with the possible exception of Io, every character in it is an immortal being. It is not as a vaunt, but as a fact, that Prometheus declares, as against Zeus (l. 1053), that "Me at least He shall never give to death."

A stupendous theological drama of which two-thirds has been lost has left an aching void, which now can never be filled, in our minds. No reader of poetry needs to be reminded of the glorious attempt of Shelley to work out a possible and worthy sequel to the *Prometheus*. Who will not echo the words of Mr. Gilbert Murray, when he says that "no piece of lost literature has been more ardently longed for than the *Prometheus Freed*"?

But, at the end of a rather prolonged attempt to understand and translate the surviving tragedies of Aeschylus, one feels inclined to repeat the words used by a powerful critic about one of the greatest of modern poets—"For man, it is a weary way to God, but a wearier far to any demigod." We shall not discover the full sequel of Aeschylus' mighty dramatic conception: we "know in part, and we prophesy in part." The Introduction (pp. xvi.-xviii.) prefixed by Mr. A. O. Prickard to his edition of the *Prometheus* is full of persuasive grace, on this topic: to him, and to Dr. Verrall of Cambridge—*lucida sidera* of help and encouragement in the study of Aeschylus—the translator's thanks are due, and are gratefully and affectionately rendered.

E. D. A. M.

THE SUPPLIANT MAIDENS

DEDICATION

Take thou this gift from out the grave of Time.
The urns of Greece lie shattered, and the cup
That for Athenian lips the Muses filled,
And flowery crowns that on Athenian hair
Hid the cicala, freedom's golden sign,
Dust in the dust have fallen. Calmly sad,
The marble dead upon Athenian tombs
Speak from their eyes "Farewell": and well have fared
They and the saddened friends, whose clasping hands
Win from the solemn stone eternity.
Yea, well they fared unto the evening god,
Passing beyond the limit of the world,
Where face to face the son his mother saw,
A living man a shadow, while she spake
Words that Odysseus and that Homer heard, —
I too, O child, I reached the common doom,
The grave, the goal of fate, and passed away.
—Such, Anticleia, as thy voice to him,
Across the dim gray gulf of death and time
Is that of Greece, a mother's to a child, —
Mother of each whose dreams are grave and fair —
Who sees the Naiad where the streams are bright
And in the sunny ripple of the sea
Cymodoce with floating golden hair:
And in the whisper of the waving oak
Hears still the Dryad's plaint, and, in the wind
That sighs through moonlit woodlands, knows the horn
Of Artemis, and silver shafts and bow.
Therefore if still around this broken vase,
Borne by rough hands, unworthy of their load,
Far from Cephisus and the wandering rills,
There cling a fragrance as of things once sweet,
Of honey from Hymettus' desert hill,
Take thou the gift and hold it close and dear;
For gifts that die have living memories —
Voices of unreturning days, that breathe
The spirit of a day that never dies.

1

ARGUMENT

Io, the daughter of Inachus, King of Argos, was beloved of Zeus. But Hera was jealous of that love, and by her ill will was Io given over to frenzy, and her body took the semblance of a heifer: and Argus, a many-eyed herdsman, was set by Hera to watch Io whithersoever she strayed. Yet, in despite of Argus, did Zeus draw nigh unto her in the shape of a bull. And by the will of Zeus and the craft of Hermes was Argus slain. Then Io was driven over far lands and seas by her madness, and came at length to the land of Egypt. There was she restored to herself by a touch of the hand of Zeus, and bare a child called Epaphus. And from Epaphus sprang Libya, and from Libya, Belus; and from Belus, Aegyptus and Danaus. And the sons of Aegyptus willed to take the daughters of Danaus in marriage. But the maidens held such wedlock in horror, and fled with their father over the sea to Argos; and the king and citizens of Argos gave them shelter and protection from their pursuers.

THE SUPPLIANT MAIDENS

DRAMATIS PERSONAE

DANAUS,
THE KING OF ARGOS,
HERALD OF AEGYPTUS.
Chorus of the Daughters of Danaus.
Attendants.

Scene. —*A sacred precinct near the gates of Argos: statue and
shrines of Zeus and other deities stand around.*

CHORUS

ZEUS! Lord and guard of suppliant hands!
Look down benign on us who crave
Thine aid—whom winds and waters drave
From where, through drifting shifting sands,
Pours Nilus to the wave.
From where the green land, god-possest,
Closes and fronts the Syrian waste,
We flee as exiles, yet unbanned
By murder's sentence from our land;
But—since Aegyptus had decreed
His sons should wed his brother's seed,—
Ourselves we tore from bonds abhorred,
From wedlock not of heart but hand,
Nor brooked to call a kinsman lord!
And Danaus, our sire and guide,
The king of counsel, pond'ring well
The dice of fortune as they fell,
Out of two griefs the kindlier chose,
And bade us fly, with him beside,
Heedless what winds or waves arose,
And o'er the wide sea waters haste,
Until to Argos' shore at last
Our wandering pinnace came—
Argos, the immemorial home
Of her from whom we boast to come—
Io, the ox-horned maiden, whom,

3

After long wandering, woe, and scathe,
Zeus with a touch, a mystic breath,
Made mother of our name.
Therefore, of all the lands of earth,
On this most gladly step we forth,
And in our hands aloft we bear—
Sole weapon for a suppliant's wear—
The olive-shoot, with wool enwound!
City, and land, and waters wan
Of Inachus, and gods most high,
And ye who, deep beneath the ground,
Bring vengeance weird on mortal man,
Powers of the grave, on you we cry!
And unto Zeus the Saviour, guard
Of mortals' holy purity!
Receive ye us—keep watch and ward
Above the suppliant maiden band!
Chaste be the heart of this your land
Towards the weak! but, ere the throng,
The wanton swarm, from Egypt sprung,
Leap forth upon the silted shore,
Thrust back their swift-rowed bark again,
Repel them, urge them to the main!
And there, 'mid storm and lightning's shine,
And scudding drift and thunder's roar,
Deep death be theirs, in stormy brine!
Before they foully grasp and win
Us, maiden-children of their kin,
And climb the couch by law denied,
And wrong each weak reluctant bride.
And now on her I call,

Mine ancestress, who far on Egypt's shore
A young cow's semblance wore,—
A maiden once, by Hera's malice changed!
And then on him withal,
Who, as amid the flowers the grazing creature
ranged,
Was in her by a breath of Zeus conceived;
And, as the hour of birth drew nigh,
By fate fulfilled, unto the light he came;
And Epaphus for name,
Born from the touch of Zeus, the child received.

4

On him, on him I cry,
And him for patron hold—
While in this grassy vale I stand,
Where Io roamed of old!
And here, recounting all her toil and pain,
Signs will I show to those who rule the land
That I am child of hers; and all shall understand,
Hearing the doubtful tale of the dim past made plain.
And, ere the end shall be,
Each man the truth of what I tell shall see.
And if there dwell hard by
One skilled to read from bird-notes augury,
That man, when through his ears shall thrill our
tearful wail,
Shall deem he hears the voice, the plaintive tale
Of her, the piteous spouse of Tereus, lord of guile—
Whom the hawk harries yet, the mourning nightingale.
She, from her happy home and fair streams scared
away,
Wails wild and sad for haunts beloved erewhile.
Yea, and for Itylus—ah, well-a-day!
Slain by her own, his mother's hand,
Maddened by lustful wrong, the deed by Tereus
planned.
Like her I wail and wail, in soft Ionian tones,
And as she wastes, even so
Wastes my soft cheek, once ripe with Nilus' suns
And all my heart dissolves in utter woe
Sad flowers of grief I cull,

Fleeing from kinsmen's love unmerciful—
Yea, from the clutching hands, the wanton crowd,
I sped across the waves, from Egypt's land of cloud[1]

[Footnote: 1: *AeRas apogas* This epithet may appear strange to
modern readers accustomed to think of Egypt as a land of cloudless
skies and pellucid atmosphere. Nevertheless both Pindar (*Pyth* iv 93)
and Apollonius Rhodius (iv 267) speak of it in the same way as
Aeschylus. It has been conjectured that they allude to the fog banks
that often obscure the low coasts—a phenomenon likely to impress
the early navigators and to be reported by them.]

Gods of the ancient cradle of my race,

Hear me, just gods! With righteous grace
On me, on me look down!
Grant not to youth its heart's unchaste desire,
But, swiftly spurning lust's unholy fire,
Bless only love and willing wedlock's crown
The war-worn fliers from the battle's wrack
Find refuge at the hallowed altar-side,
The sanctuary divine, —
Ye gods! such refuge unto me provide —
Such sanctuary be mine!
Though the deep will of Zeus be hard to track,
Yet doth it flame and glance,
A beacon in the dark, 'mid clouds of chance
That wrap mankind
Yea, though the counsel fall, undone it shall not be,
Whate'er be shaped and fixed within Zeus' ruling mind —
Dark as a solemn grove, with sombre leafage shaded,
His paths of purpose wind,
A marvel to man's eye

Smitten by him, from towering hopes degraded,
Mortals lie low and still
Tireless and effortless, works forth its will
The arm divine!
God from His holy seat, in calm of unarmed power,
Brings forth the deed, at its appointed hour!
Let Him look down on mortal wantonness!
Lo! how the youthful stock of Belus' line
Craves for me, uncontrolled —
With greed and madness bold —
Urged on by passion's sunless stress —
And, cheated, learns too late the prey has 'scaped
their hold!
Ah, listen, listen to my grievous tale,
My sorrow's words, my shrill and tearful cries!
Ah woe, ah woe!
Loud with lament the accents use,
And from my living lips my own sad dirges flow!
O Apian land of hill and dale,
Thou kennest yet, O land, this faltered foreign wail —
Have mercy, hear my prayer!
Lo, how again, again, I rend and tear
My woven raiment, and from off my hair

Cast the Sidonian veil!

Ah, but if fortune smile, if death be driven away,
Vowed rites, with eager haste, we to the gods will pay!
Alas, alas again!
O wither drift the waves? and who shall loose the pain?

O Apian land of hill and dale,
Thou kennest yet, O land, this faltered foreign wail!
Have mercy, hear my prayer!
Lo, how again, again, I rend and tear
My woven raiment, and from off my hair
Cast the Sidonian veil!

The wafting oar, the bark with woven sail,
From which the sea foamed back,
Sped me, unharmed of storms, along the breeze's track—
Be it unblamed of me!
But ah, the end, the end of my emprise!
May He, the Father, with all-seeing eyes,
Grant me that end to see!
Grant that henceforth unstained as heretofore
I may escape the forced embrace
Of those proud children of the race
That sacred Io bore.

And thou, O maiden-goddess chaste and pure—
Queen of the inner fane,—
Look of thy grace on me, O Artemis,
Thy willing suppliant—thine, thine it is,
Who from the lustful onslaught fled secure,
To grant that I too without stain
The shelter of thy purity may gain!

Grant that henceforth unstained as heretofore
I may escape the forced embrace
Of those proud children of the race
That sacred Io bore!

Yet if this may not be,
We, the dark race sun-smitten, we
Will speed with suppliant wands
To Zeus who rules below, with hospitable hands

Who welcomes all the dead from all the lands:
Yea by our own hands strangled, we will go,
Spurned by Olympian gods, unto the gods below!

Zeus, hear and save!
The searching, poisonous hate, that Io vexed and drave,
Was of a goddess: well I know
The bitter ire, the wrathful woe
Of Hera, queen of heaven—-
A storm, a storm her breath, whereby we yet are driven!
Bethink thee, what dispraise
Of Zeus himself mankind will raise,
If now he turn his face averted from our cries!
If now, dishonoured and alone,
The ox-horned maiden's race shall be undone,
Children of Epaphus, his own begotten son—-
Zeus, listen from on high!—to thee our prayers arise.

Zeus, hear and save!
The searching poisonous hate, that Io vexed and drave,
Was of a goddess: well I know
The bitter ire, the wrathful woe
Of Hera, queen of heaven—
A storm, a storm her breath, whereby we yet are driven!

DANAUS

Children, be wary—wary he with whom
Ye come, your trusty sire and steersman old:
And that same caution hold I here on land,
And bid you hoard my words, inscribing them
On memory's tablets. Lo, I see afar
Dust, voiceless herald of a host, arise;
And hark, within their grinding sockets ring
Axles of hurrying wheels! I see approach,
Borne in curved cars, by speeding horses drawn,
A speared and shielded band. The chiefs, perchance,
Of this their land are hitherward intent
To look on us, of whom they yet have heard
By messengers alone. But come who may,
And come he peaceful or in ravening wrath
Spurred on his path, 'twere best, in any case,
Damsels, to cling unto this altar-mound
Made sacred to their gods of festival,—
A shrine is stronger than a tower to save,
A shield that none may cleave. Step swift thereto,
And in your left hands hold with reverence
The white-crowned wands of suppliance, the sign
Beloved of Zeus, compassion's lord, and speak
To those that question you, words meek and low
And piteous, as beseems your stranger state,
Clearly avowing of this flight of yours
The bloodless cause; and on your utterance
See to it well that modesty attend;
From downcast eyes, from brows of pure control,
Let chastity look forth; nor, when ye speak,
Be voluble nor eager—they that dwell
Within this land are sternly swift to chide.
And be your words submissive: heed this well;
For weak ye are, outcasts on stranger lands,
And froward talk beseems not strengthless hands.

CHORUS

O father, warily to us aware
Thy words are spoken, and thy wisdom's best
My mind shall hoard, with Zeus our sire to aid.

DANAUS

Even so—with gracious aspect let him aid.

CHORUS

Fain were I now to seat me by thy side.

DANAUS

Now dally not, but put our thought in act.

CHORUS

Zeus, pity our distress, or e'er we die.

DANAUS

If so he will, your toils to joy will turn.

CHORUS

Lo, on this shrine, the semblance of a bird.[2]

DANAUS

Zeus' bird of dawn it is; invoke the sign.

CHORUS

Thus I invoke the saving rays of morn.

[Footnote: 2: The whole of this dialogue in alternate verses is
disarranged in the MSS. The re-arrangement which has approved
itself
to Paley has been here followed. It involves, however, a hiatus,
instead of the line to which this note is appended. The substance of
the lost line being easily deducible from the context, it has been
supplied in the translation.]

DANAUS

Next, bright Apollo, exiled once from heaven.

CHORUS

The exiled god will pity our exile.

DANAUS

Yea, may he pity, giving grace and aid.

CHORUS

Whom next invoke I, of these other gods?

DANAUS

Lo, here a trident, symbol of a god.

CHORUS

Who [3] gave sea-safety; may he bless on land!
[Footnote: 3: Poseidon] DANAUS

This next is Hermes, carved in Grecian wise.

CHORUS

Then let him herald help to freedom won.

DANAUS

Lastly, adore this altar consecrate
To many lesser gods in one; then crouch
On holy ground, a flock of doves that flee,
Scared by no alien hawks, a kin not kind,
Hateful, and fain of love more hateful still.
Foul is the bird that rends another bird,
And foul the men who hale unwilling maids,
From sire unwilling, to the bridal bed.
Never on earth, nor in the lower world,
Shall lewdness such as theirs escape the ban:
There too, if men say right, a God there is
Who upon dead men turns their sin to doom,
To final doom. Take heed, draw hitherward,
That from this hap your safety ye may win.
[*Enter the* KING OF ARGOS.

THE KING OF ARGOS

Speak—of what land are ye? No Grecian band
Is this to whom I speak, with Eastern robes
And wrappings richly dight: no Argive maid,
No woman in all Greece such garb doth wear.
This too gives marvel, how unto this land,
Unheralded, unfriended, without guide,
And without fear, ye came? yet wands I see,
True sign of suppliance, by you laid down
On shrines of these our gods of festival.
No land but Greece can read such signs aright.
Much else there is, conjecture well might guess,
But let words teach the man who stands to hear.

CHORUS

True is the word thou spakest of my garb;
But speak I unto thee as citizen,
Or Hermes' wandbearer, or chieftain king?

THE KING OF ARGOS

For that, take heart and answer without fear.
I am Pelasgus, ruler of this land,
Child of Palaichthon, whom the earth brought forth;
And, rightly named from me, the race who reap
This country's harvests are Pelasgian called.
And o'er the wide and westward-stretching land,
Through which the lucent wave of Strymon flows
I rule; Perrhaebia's land my boundary is
Northward, and Pindus' further slopes, that watch
Paeonia, and Dodona's mountain ridge.
West, east, the limit of the washing seas
Restrains my rule—the interspace is mine.
But this whereon we stand is Apian land,
Styled so of old from the great healer's name;
For Apis, coming from Naupactus' shore
Beyond the strait, child of Apollo's self
And like him seer and healer, cleansed this land
From man-devouring monsters, whom the earth,
Stained with pollution of old bloodshedding,
Brought forth in malice, beasts of ravening jaws,
A grisly throng of serpents manifold.
And healings of their hurt, by knife and charm,
Apis devised, unblamed of Argive men,
And in their prayers found honour, for reward.
—Lo, thou hast heard the tokens that I give:
Speak now thy race, and tell a forthright tale;
In sooth, this people loves not many words.

CHORUS

Short is my word and clear. Of Argive race
We come, from her, the ox-horned maiden who
Erst bare the sacred child. My word shall give
Whate'er can 'stablish this my soothfast tale.

THE KING OF ARGOS

O stranger maids, I may not trust this word,
That ye have share in this our Argive race.
No likeness of our country do ye bear,
But semblance as of Libyan womankind.
Even such a stock by Nilus' banks might grow;
Yea and the Cyprian stamp, in female forms,
Shows to the life, what males impressed the same.
And, furthermore, of roving Indian maids
Whose camping-grounds by Aethiopia lie,
And camels burdened even as mules, and bearing
Riders, as horses bear, mine ears have heard;
And tales of flesh-devouring mateless maids
Called Amazons: to these, if bows ye bare,
I most had deemed you like. Speak further yet,
That of your Argive birth the truth I learn.

CHORUS

Here in this Argive land—so runs the tale—
Io was priestess once of Hera's fane.

THE KING OF ARGOS

Yea, truth it is, and far this word prevails:
Is't said that Zeus with mortal mingled love?

CHORUS

Ay, and that Hera that embrace surmised.

THE KING OF ARGOS

How issued then this strife of those on high?

CHORUS

By Hera's will, a heifer she became.

THE KING OF ARGOS

Held Zeus aloof then from the horned beast?

CHORUS

'Tis said, he loved, in semblance of a bull.

THE KING OF ARGOS

And his stern consort, did she aught thereon?

CHORUS

One myriad-eyed she set, the heifer's guard.

THE KING OF ARGOS

How namest thou this herdsman many-eyed?

CHORUS

Argus, the child of Earth, whom Hermes slew.

THE KING OF ARGOS

Still did the goddess vex the beast ill-starred?

CHORUS

She wrought a gadfly with a goading sting.

THE KING OF ARGOS

Thus drave she Io hence, to roam afar?

CHORUS

Yea—this thy word coheres exact with mine.

THE KING OF ARGOS

Then to Canopus and to Memphis came she?

CHORUS

And by Zeus' hand was touched, and bare a child.

THE KING OF ARGOS

Who vaunts him the Zeus-mated creature's son?

CHORUS

Epaphus, named rightly from the saving touch.

THE KING OF ARGOS

And whom in turn did Epaphus beget?[4]

[Footnote: 4: Here one verse at least has been lost. The conjecture of
Bothe seems to be verified, as far as substance is concerned, by the
next line, and has consequently been adopted.]

CHORUS

Libya, with name of a wide land endowed.

THE KING OF ARGOS

And who from her was born unto the race?

CHORUS

Belus: from him two sons, my father one.

THE KING OF ARGOS

Speak now to me his name, this greybeard wise.

CHORUS

Revere the gods thus crowned, who steer the State.

THE KING OF ARGOS

Awe thrills me, seeing these shrines with leafage crowned.

CHORUS

Yea, stern the wrath of Zeus, the suppliants' lord.
Child of Palaichthon, royal chief
Of thy Pelasgians, hear!
Bow down thine heart to my relief—
A fugitive, a suppliant, swift with fear,
A creature whom the wild wolves chase
O'er toppling crags; in piteous case
Aloud, afar she lows,
Calling the herdsman's trusty arm to save her from her foes!

THE KING OF ARGOS

Lo, with bowed heads beside our city shrines
Ye sit 'neath shade of new-plucked olive-boughs.
Our distant kin's resentment Heaven forefend!
Let not this hap, unhoped and unforeseen,
Bring war on us: for strife we covet not.

CHORUS

Justice, the daughter of right-dealing Zeus,
Justice, the queen of suppliants, look down,
That this our plight no ill may loose
Upon your town!
This word, even from the young, let age and wisdom learn:
If thou to suppliants show grace,
Thou shalt not lack Heaven's grace in turn,
So long as virtue's gifts on heavenly shrines have place.

THE KING OF ARGOS

Not at my private hearth ye sit and sue;
And if the city bear a common stain,
Be it the common toil to cleanse the same:
Therefore no pledge, no promise will I give,
Ere counsel with the commonwealth be held.

CHORUS

Nay, but the source of sway, the city's self, art thou,
A power unjudged! thine, only thine,
To rule the right of hearth and shrine!
Before thy throne and sceptre all men bow!
Thou, in all causes lord, beware the curse divine!

THE KING OF ARGOS

May that curse fall upon mine enemies!
I cannot aid you without risk of scathe,
Nor scorn your prayers—unmerciful it were.
Perplexed, distraught I stand, and fear alike
The twofold chance, to do or not to do.

CHORUS

Have heed of him who looketh from on high,
The guard of woeful mortals, whosoe'er
Unto their fellows cry,
And find no pity, find no justice there.
Abiding in his wrath, the suppliants' lord
Doth smite, unmoved by cries, unbent by prayerful word.

THE KING OF ARGOS

But if Aegyptus' children grasp you here,
Claiming, their country's right, to hold you theirs
As next of kin, who dares to counter this?
Plead ye your country's laws, if plead ye may,
That upon you they lay no lawful hand.

CHORUS

Let me not fall, O nevermore,
A prey into the young men's hand;
Rather than wed whom I abhor,
By pilot-stars I flee this land;
O king, take justice to thy side,
And with the righteous powers decide!

THE KING OF ARGOS

Hard is the cause—make me not judge thereof.
Already I have vowed it, to do nought
Save after counsel with my people ta'en,
King though I be; that ne'er in after time,
If ill fate chance, my people then may say—
In aid of strangers thou the state hast slain.

CHORUS

Zeus, lord of kinship, rules at will
The swaying balance, and surveys
Evil and good; to men of ill
Gives evil, and to good men praise.
And thou—since true those scales do sway—
Shall thou from justice shrink away?

THE KING OF ARGOS

A deep, a saving counsel here there needs—
An eye that like a diver to the depth
Of dark perplexity can pass and see,
Undizzied, unconfused. First must we care
That to the State and to ourselves this thing
Shall bring no ruin; next, that wrangling hands
Shall grasp you not as prey, nor we ourselves
Betray you thus embracing sacred shrines,
Nor make the avenging all-destroying god,
Who not in hell itself sets dead men free,
A grievous inmate, an abiding bane.—
Spake I not right, of saving counsel's need?

CHORUS

Yea, counsel take and stand to aid
At Justice' side and mine.
Betray not me, the timorous maid
Whom far beyond the brine
A godless violence cast forth forlorn.
O King, wilt thou behold —
Lord of this land, wilt thou behold me torn
From altars manifold?
Bethink thee of the young men's wrath and lust,
Hold off their evil pride;
Steel not thyself to see the suppliant thrust
From hallowed statues' side,
Haled by the frontlet on my forehead bound,
As steeds are led, and drawn
By hands that drag from shrine and altar-mound
My vesture's fringed lawn.
Know thou that whether for Aegyptus' race
Thou dost their wish fulfil,
Or for the gods and for each holy place —
Be thy choice good or ill,
Blow is with blow requited, grace with grace
Such is Zeus' righteous will.

THE KING OF ARGOS

Yea, I have pondered: from the sea of doubt
Here drives at length the bark of thought ashore;
Landward with screw and windlass haled, and firm,
Clamped to her props, she lies. The need is stern;
With men or gods a mighty strife we strive
Perforce, and either hap in grief concludes.
For, if a house be sacked, new wealth for old
Not hard it is to win—if Zeus the lord
Of treasure favour—more than quits the loss,
Enough to pile the store of wealth full high;
Or if a tongue shoot forth untimely speech,
Bitter and strong to goad a man to wrath,
Soft words there be to soothe that wrath away:
But what device shall make the war of kin
Bloodless? that woe, the blood of many beasts,
And victims manifold to many gods,
Alone can cure. Right glad I were to shun
This strife, and am more fain of ignorance
Than of the wisdom of a woe endured.
The gods send better than my soul foretells!

CHORUS

Of many cries for mercy, hear the end.

THE KING OF ARGOS

Say on, then, for it shall not 'scape mine ear.

CHORUS

Girdles we have, and bands that bind our robes.

THE KING OF ARGOS

Even so; such things beseem a woman's wear.

CHORUS

Know, then, with these a fair device there is—

THE KING OF ARGOS

Speak, then: what utterance doth this foretell?

CHORUS

Unless to us thou givest pledge secure—

THE KING OF ARGOS

What can thy girdles' craft achieve for thee?

CHORUS

Strange votive tablets shall these statues deck.

THE KING OF ARGOS

Mysterious thy resolve—avow it clear.

CHORUS

Swiftly to hang me on these sculptured gods!

THE KING OF ARGOS

Thy word is as a lash to urge my heart.

CHORUS

Thou seest truth, for I have cleared thine eye

THE KING OF ARGOS

Yea, and woes manifold, invincible,
A crowd of ills, sweep on me torrent-like.
My bark goes forth upon a sea of troubles
Unfathomed, ill to traverse, harbourless.
For if my deed shall match not your demand,
Dire, beyond shot of speech, shall be the bane
Your death's pollution leaves unto this land.
Yet if against your kin, Aegyptus' race,
Before our gates I front the doom of war,
Will not the city's loss be sore? Shall men
For women's sake incarnadine the ground?
But yet the wrath of Zeus, the suppliants' lord
I needs must fear: most awful unto man
The terror of his anger. Thou, old man,
The father of these maidens, gather up
Within your arms these wands of suppliance,
And lay them at the altars manifold
Of all our country's gods, that all the town
Know, by this sign, that ye come here to sue.
Nor, in thy haste, do thou say aught of me.
Swift is this folk to censure those who rule;
But, if they see these signs of suppliance,
It well may chance that each will pity you,
And loathe the young men's violent pursuit;
And thus a fairer favour you may find:
For, to the helpless, each man's heart is kind.

DANAUS

To us, beyond gifts manifold it is
To find a champion thus compassionate;
Yet send with me attendants, of thy folk,
Rightly to guide me, that I duly find
Each altar of your city's gods that stands
Before the fane, each dedicated shrine;
And that in safety through the city's ways
I may pass onwards: all unlike to yours
The outward semblance that I wear—the race
that Nilus rears is all dissimilar
That of Inachus. Keep watch and ward
Lest heedlessness bring death: full oft, I ween,
Friend hath slain friend, not knowing whom he slew.

THE KING OF ARGOS

Go at his side, attendants,—he saith well.
On to the city's consecrated shrines!
Nor be of many words to those ye meet,
The while this suppliant voyager ye lead.
[*Exit* DANAUS *with attendants.*

CHORUS

Let him go forward, thy command obeying.
But me how biddest, how assurest thou?

THE KING OF ARGOS

Leave there the new-plucked boughs, thy sorrow's sign.

CHORUS

Thus beckoned forth, at thy behest I leave them.

THE KING OF ARGOS

Now to this level precinct turn thyself.

CHORUS

Unconsecrate it is, and cannot shield me.

THE KING OF ARGOS

We will not yield thee to those falcons' greed.

CHORUS

What help? more fierce they are than serpents fell

THE KING OF ARGOS

We spake thee fair—speak thou them fair in turn.

CHORUS

What marvel that we loathe them, scared in soul?

THE KING OF ARGOS

Awe towards a king should other fears transcend.

CHORUS

Thus speak, thus act, and reassure my mind.

THE KING OF ARGOS

Not long thy sire shall leave thee desolate.
But I will call the country's indwellers,
And with soft words th' assembly will persuade,
And warn your sire what pleadings will avail.
Therefore abide ye, and with prayer entreat
The country's gods to compass your desire;
The while I go, this matter to provide,
Persuasion and fair fortune at my side.
[*Exit the* KING OF ARGOS.

CHORUS

O King of Kings, among the blest
Thou highest and thou happiest,
Listen and grant our prayer,
And, deeply loathing, thrust
Away from us the young men's lust,
And deeply drown
In azure waters, down and ever down,
Benches and rowers dark,
The fatal and perfidious bark!
Unto the maidens turn thy gracious care;
Think yet again upon the tale of fame,
How from the maiden loved of thee there sprung
Mine ancient line, long since in many a legend sung!
Remember, O remember, thou whose hand
Did Io by a touch to human shape reclaim.
For from this Argos erst our mother came
Driven hence to Egypt's land,
Yet sprung of Zeus we were, and hence our birth we claim.
And now have I roamed back
Unto the ancient track
Where Io roamed and pastured among flowers,
Watched o'er by Argus' eyes,
Through the lush grasses and the meadow bowers.
Thence, by the gadfly maddened, forth she flies
Unto far lands and alien peoples driven
And, following fate, through paths of foam and surge,
Sees, as she goes, the cleaving strait divide
Greece, from the Eastland riven.
And swift through Asian borders doth she urge
Her course, o'er Phrygian mountains' sheep-clipt side;
Thence, where the Mysian realm of Teuthras lies
Towards Lydian lowlands hies,
And o'er Cilician and Pamphylian hills
And ever-flowing rills,
And thence to Aphrodite's fertile shore, [5]
[Footnote: 5: Cyprus.]
The land of garnered wheat and wealthy store
And thence, deep-stung by wild unrest,
By the winged fly that goaded her and drave,
Unto the fertile land, the god-possest,
(Where, fed from far-off snows,

Life-giving Nilus flows,
Urged on by Typho's strength, a fertilizing wave)
She roves, in harassed and dishonoured flight
Scathed by the blasting pangs of Hera's dread despite.
And they within the land
With terror shook and wanned,
So strange the sight they saw, and were afraid—
A wild twy-natured thing, half heifer and half maid.
Whose hand was laid at last on Io, thus forlorn,
With many roamings worn?
Who bade the harassed maiden's peace return?
Zeus, lord of time eterne.
Yea, by his breath divine, by his unscathing strength,
She lays aside her bane,
And softened back to womanhood at length
Sheds human tears again.
Then, quickened with Zeus' veritable seed,
A progeny she bare,
A stainless babe, a child of heavenly breed.
Of life and fortune fair.
His is the life of life—so all men say,—
His is the seed of Zeus.
Who else had power stern Hera's craft to stay,
Her vengeful curse to loose?

Yea, all from Zeus befell!
And rightly wouldst thou tell
That we from Epaphus, his child, were born:
Justly his deed was done;
Unto what other one,
Of all the gods, should I for justice turn?
From him our race did spring;
Creator he and King,
Ancient of days and wisdom he, and might.
As bark before the wind,
So, wafted by his mind,
Moves every counsel, each device aright.
Beneath no stronger hand
Holds he a weak command,
No throne doth he abase him to adore;
Swift as a word, his deed
Acts out what stands decreed
In counsels of his heart, for evermore.

[*Re-enter* DANAUS.

DANAUS

Take heart, my children: the land's heart is kind,
And to full issue has their voting come.

CHORUS

All hail, my sire; thy word brings utmost joy.
Say, to what issue is the vote made sure,
And how prevailed the people's crowding hands?

DANAUS

With one assent the Argives spake their will,
And, hearing, my old heart took youthful cheer,
The very sky was thrilled when high in air
The concourse raised right hands and swore their oath:—
Free shall the maidens sojourn in this land.
Unharried, undespoiled by mortal wight:
No native hand, no hand of foreigner
Shall drag them hence; if any man use force—
Whoe'er of all our countrymen shall fail
To come unto their aid, let him go forth,
Beneath the people's curse, to banishment.
So did the king of this Pelasgian folk
Plead on behalf of us, and bade them heed
That never, in the after-time, this realm
Should feed to fulness the great enmity
Of Zeus, the suppliants' guard, against itself!
A twofold curse, for wronging stranger-guests
Who are akin withal, confrontingly
Should rise before this city and be shown
A ruthless monster, fed on human doom.
Such things the Argive people heard, and straight,
Without proclaim of herald, gave assent:
Yea, in full conclave, the Pelasgian folk
Heard suasive pleas, and Zeus through them resolved.

CHORUS

Arouse we now to chant our prayer
For fair return of service fair
And Argos' kindly will.
Zeus, lord of guestright, look upon
The grace our stranger lips have won.
In right and truth, as they begun,
Guide them, with favouring hand, until
Thou dost their blameless wish fulfil!

Now may the Zeus-born gods on high
Hear us pour forth
A votive prayer for Argos' clan!—
Never may this Pelasgian earth,
Amid the fire-wrack, shrill the dismal cry
On Ares, ravening lord of fight,
Who in an alien harvest mows down man!
For lo, this land had pity on our plight,
And unto us were merciful and leal,
To us, the piteous flock, who at Zeus' altar kneel!
They scorned not the pleas of maidenhood,
Nor with the young men's will hath their will stood.
They knew right well.

Th' unearthly watching fiend invincible,
The foul avenger—let him not draw near!
For he, on roofs ill-starred,
Defiling and polluting, keeps a ghastly ward!
They knew his vengeance, and took holy heed
To us, the sister suppliants, who cry
To Zeus, the lord of purity:
Therefore with altars pure they shall the gods revere.

Thus, through the boughs that shade our lips, fly forth in air,
Fly forth, O eager prayer!
May never pestilence efface
This city's race,
Nor be the land with corpses strewed,
Nor stained with civic blood!
The stem of youth, unpluckt, to manhood come,
Nor Ares rise from Aphrodite's bower,
The lord of death and bane, to waste our youthful flower.

Long may the old
Crowd to the altars kindled to consume
Gifts rich and manifold —
Offered to win from powers divine
A benison on city and on shrine:
Let all the sacred might adore
Of Zeus most high, the lord
Of guestright and the hospitable board,
Whose immemorial law doth rule Fate's scales aright:
The garners of earth's store
Be full for evermore,
And grace of Artemis make women's travail light;
No devastating curse of fell disease
This city seize;
No clamour of the State arouse to war
Ares, from whom afar
Shrinketh the lute, by whom the dances fail —
Ares, the lord of wail.
Swarm far aloof from Argos' citizens
All plague and pestilence,
And may the Archer-God our children spare!
May Zeus with foison and with fruitfulness
The land's each season bless,
And, quickened with Heaven's bounty manifold,
Teem grazing flock and fold.
Beside the altars of Heaven's hallowing
Loud let the minstrels sing,
And from pure lips float forth the harp-led strain in air!
And let the people's voice, the power
That sways the State, in danger's hour
Be wary, wise for all;
Nor honour in dishonour hold,
But — ere the voice of war be bold —
Let them to stranger peoples grant
Fair and unbloody covenant —
Justice and peace withal;
And to the Argive powers divine
The sacrifice of laurelled kine,
By rite ancestral, pay.
Among three words of power and awe,
Stands this, the third, the mighty law —
Your gods, your fathers deified,
Ye shall adore. Let this abide

For ever and for aye.

DANAUS

Dear children, well and wisely have ye prayed;
I bid you now not shudder, though ye hear
New and alarming tidings from your sire.
From this high place beside the suppliants' shrine
The bark of our pursuers I behold,
By divers tokens recognized too well.
Lo, the spread canvas and the hides that screen
The gunwale; lo, the prow, with painted eyes
That seem her onward pathway to descry,
Heeding too well the rudder at the stern
That rules her, coming for no friendly end.
And look, the seamen—all too plain their race—
Their dark limbs gleam from out their snow-white garb;
Plain too the other barks, a fleet that comes
All swift to aid the purpose of the first,
That now, with furled sail and with pulse of oars
Which smite the wave together, comes aland.
But ye, be calm, and, schooled not scared by fear,
Confront this chance, be mindful of your trust
In these protecting gods. And I will hence,
And champions who shall plead your cause aright
Will bring unto your side. There come perchance
Heralds or envoys, eager to lay hand
And drag you captive hence; yet fear them not;
Foiled shall they be. Yet well it were for you
(If, ere with aid I come, I tarry long),
Not by one step this sanctuary to leave.
Farewell, fear nought: soon shall the hour be born
When he that scorns the gods shall rue his scorn

CHORUS

Ah but I shudder, father!—ah, even now,
Even as I speak, the swift-winged ships draw nigh!

I shudder, I shiver, I perish with fear:
Overseas though I fled,
Yet nought it avails; my pursuers are near!

31

DANAUS

Children, take heart; they who decreed to aid
Thy cause will arm for battle, well I ween.

CHORUS

But desperate is Aegyptus' ravening race,
With fight unsated; thou too know'st it well.

In their wrath they o'ertake us; the prow is deep-dark
In the which they have sped,
And dark is the bench and the crew of the bark!

DANAUS

Yea but a crew as stout they here shall find,
And arms well steeled beneath a noon-day sun.

CHORUS

Ah yet, O father, leave us not forlorn!
Alone, a maid is nought, a strengthless arm.
With guile they Pursue me, with counsel malign,
And unholy their soul;
And as ravens they seize me, unheeding the shrine!

DANAUS

Fair will befall us, children, in this chance,
If thus in wrath they wrong the gods and you.

CHORUS

Alas, nor tridents nor the sanctity
Of shrines will drive them, O my sire, from us!

Unholy and daring and cursed is their ire,
Nor own they control
Of the gods, but like jackals they glut their desire!

DANAUS

Ay, but *Come wolf, flee jackal,* saith the saw;
Nor can the flax-plant overbear the corn.

CHORUS

Lustful, accursed, monstrous is their will
As of beasts ravening—'ware we of their power!

DANAUS

Look you, not swiftly puts a fleet to sea,
Nor swiftly to its moorings; long it is
Or e'er the saving cables to the shore
Are borne, and long or e'er the steersmen cry,
The good ship swings at anchor—all is well.
Longest of all, the task to come aland
Where haven there is none, when sunset fades
In night. *To pilot wise,* the adage saith,
Night is a day of wakefulness and pain.
Therefore no force of weaponed men, as yet
Scatheless can come ashore, before the bank
Lie at her anchorage securely moored.
Bethink thee therefore, nor in panic leave
The shrine of gods whose succour thou hast won
I go for aid—men shall not blame me long,
Old, but with youth at heart and on my tongue
[*Exit* DANAUS.

CHORUS

O land of hill and dale, O holy land,
What shall befall us? whither shall we flee,
From Apian land to some dark lair of earth?

O would that in vapour of smoke I might rise to the clouds of the sky,
That as dust which flits up without wings I might pass and evanish and die!
I dare not, I dare not abide: my heart yearns, eager to fly;
And dark is the cast of my thought; I shudder and tremble for fear.
My father looked forth and beheld: I die of the sight that draws near.

And for me be the strangling cord, the halter made ready by Fate,
Before to my body draws nigh the man of my horror and hate.
Nay, ere I will own him as lord, as handmaid to Hades I go!
And oh, that aloft in the sky, where the dark clouds are frozen to snow,
A refuge for me might be found, or a mountain-top smooth and too high

For the foot of the goat, where the vulture sits lonely,
and none may descry
The pinnacle veiled in the cloud,
the highest and sheerest of all,
Ere to wedlock that rendeth my heart,
and love that is loveless, I fall!
Yea, a prey to the dogs and the birds of the mount
will I give me to be, —
From wailing and curse and pollution it is death,
only death, sets me free:
Let death come upon me before
to the ravisher's bed I am thrust;
What champion, what saviour but death can I find,
or what refuge from lust?
I will utter my shriek of entreaty,
a prayer that shrills up to the sky,
That calleth the gods to compassion,
a tuneful, a pitiful cry,
That is loud to invoke the releaser.
O father, look down on the fight;
Look down in thy wrath on the wronger,
with eyes that are eager for right.
Zeus, thou that art lord of the world,
whose kingdom is strong over all,
Have mercy on us! At thine altar for refuge
and safety we call.
For the race of Aegyptus is fierce,
with greed and with malice afire;
They cry as the questing hounds,
they sweep with the speed of desire.
But thine is the balance of fate,
thou rulest the wavering scale,
And without thee no mortal emprise
shall have strength to achieve or prevail.

Alack, alack! the ravisher—
He leaps from boat to beach, he draweth near!
Away, thou plunderer accurst!
Death seize thee first,
Or e'er thou touch me—off! God, hear our cry,
Our maiden agony!
Ah, ah, the touch, the prelude of my shame.
Alas, my maiden fame!
O sister, sister, to the altar cling,
For he that seizeth me,
Grim is his wrath and stern, by land as on the sea.
Guard us, O king!
[*Enter the* HERALD OF AEGYPTUS]

HERALD OF AEGYPTUS

Hence to my barge—step swiftly, tarry not.

CHORUS

Alack, he rends—he rends my hair! O wound on
wound!
Help! my lopped head will fall, my blood gush o'er
the ground!

HERALD OF AEGYPTUS

Aboard, ye cursed—with a new curse, go!

CHORUS

Would God that on the wand'ring brine
Thou and this braggart tongue of thine
Had sunk beneath the main—
Thy mast and planks, made fast in vain!
Thee would I drive aboard once more,
A slayer and a dastard, from the shore!

HERALD OF AEGYPTUS

Be still, thou vain demented soul;
My force thy craving shall control.
Away, aboard! What, clingest to the shrine?
Away! this city's gods I hold not for divine.

CHORUS

Aid me, ye gods, that never, never
I may again behold
The mighty, the life-giving river,
Nilus, the quickener of field and fold!
Alack, O sire, unto the shrine I cling—
Shrine of this land from which mine ancient line did spring!

HERALD OF AEGYPTUS

Shrines, shrines, forsooth!—the ship, the ship be shrine!
Aboard, perforce and will-ye nill-ye, go!
Or e'er from hands of mine
Ye suffer torments worse and blow on blow.

CHORUS

Alack, God grant those hands may strive in vain
With the salt-streaming wave,
When 'gainst the wide-blown blasts thy bark shall strain
To round Sarpedon's cape, the sandbank's treach'rous grave.

HERALD OF AEGYPTUS

Shrill ye and shriek unto what gods ye may,
Ye shall not leap from out Aegyptus' bark,
How bitterly soe'er ye wail your woe.

CHORUS

Alack, alack my wrong!
Stern is thy voice, thy vaunting loud and strong.
Thy sire, the mighty Nilus, drive thee hence
Turning to death and doom thy greedy violence!

HERALD OF AEGYPTUS

Swift to the vessel of the double prow,
Go quickly! let none linger, else this hand
Ruthless will hale you by your tresses hence.

CHORUS

Alack, O father! from the shrine
Not aid but agony is mine.
As a spider he creeps and he clutches his prey,
And he hales me away.
A spectre of darkness, of darkness. Alas and alas! well-a-day!
O Earth, O my mother! O Zeus, thou king of the earth, and her child!
Turn back, we pray thee, from us his clamour and threatenings wild!

HERALD OF AEGYPTUS

Peace! I fear not this country's deities.
They fostered not my childhood nor mine age.

CHORUS

Like a snake that is human he comes,
he shudders and crawls to my side;
As an adder that biteth the foot,
his clutch on my flesh doth abide.
O Earth, O my mother! O Zeus, thou king of the earth,
and her child!
Turn back, we pray thee, from us his clamour
and threatenings wild!

HERALD OF AEGYPTUS

Swift each unto the ship; repine no more,
Or my hand shall not spare to rend your robe.

CHORUS

O chiefs, O leaders, aid me, or I yield!

HERALD OF AEGYPTUS

Peace! if ye have not ears to hear my words,
Lo, by these tresses must I hale you hence.

CHORUS

Undone we are, O king! all hope is gone.

HERALD OF AEGYPTUS

Ay, kings enow ye shall behold anon,
Aegyptus' sons—Ye shall not want for kings.
[*Enter the* KING OF ARGOS.

THE KING OF ARGOS

Sirrah, what dost thou? in what arrogance
Darest thou thus insult Pelasgia's realm?
Deemest thou this a woman-hearted town?
Thou art too full of thy barbarian scorn
For us of Grecian blood, and, erring thus,
Thou dost bewray thyself a fool in all!

HERALD OF AEGYPTUS

Say thou wherein my deeds transgress my right.

THE KING OF ARGOS

First, that thou play'st a stranger's part amiss.

HERALD OF AEGYPTUS

Wherein? I do but search and claim mine own.

THE KING OF ARGOS

To whom of our guest-champions hast appealed?

HERALD OF AEGYPTUS

To Hermes, herald's champion, lord of search.

THE KING OF ARGOS

Yea, to a god—yet dost thou wrong the gods!

HERALD OF AEGYPTUS

The gods that rule by Nilus I revere.

THE KING OF ARGOS

Hear I aright? our Argive gods are nought?

HERALD OF AEGYPTUS

The prey is mine, unless force rend it from me.

THE KING OF ARGOS

At thine own peril touch them—'ware, and soon!

HERALD OF AEGYPTUS

I hear thy speech, no hospitable word.

THE KING OF ARGOS

I am no host for sacrilegious hands.

HERALD OF AEGYPTUS

I will go tell this to Aegyptus' sons.

THE KING OF ARGOS

Tell it! my pride will ponder not thy word.

HERALD OF AEGYPTUS

Yet, that I have my message clear to say
(For it behooves that heralds' words be clear,
Be they or ill or good), how art thou named?
By whom despoiled of this sister-band
Of maidens pass I homeward?—speak and say!
For lo, henceforth in Ares' court we stand,
Who judges not by witness but by war:
No pledge of silver now can bring the cause
To issue: ere this thing end, there must be
Corpse piled on corpse and many lives gasped forth.

THE KING OF ARGOS

What skills it that I tell my name to thee?
Thou and thy mates shall learn it ere the end.
Know that if words unstained by violence
Can change these maidens' choice, then mayest thou,
With full consent of theirs, conduct them hence.
But thus the city with one voice ordained—

No force shall bear away the maiden band.

Firmly this word upon the temple wall
Is by a rivet clenched, and shall abide:
Not upon wax inscribed and delible,
Nor upon parchment sealed and stored away.—
Lo, thou hast heard our free mouths speak their will:
Out from our presence—tarry not, but go!

HERALD OF AEGYPTUS

Methinks we stand on some new edge of war:
Be strength and triumph on the young men's side!

THE KING OF ARGOS

Nay but here also shall ye find young men,
Unsodden with the juices oozed from grain.[6]
[*Exit* HERALD OF AEGYPTUS
But ye, O maids, with your attendants true,
Pass hence with trust into the fenced town,
Ringed with a wide confine of guarding towers.
Therein are many dwellings for such guests
As the State honours; there myself am housed
Within a palace neither scant nor strait.
There dwell ye, if ye will to lodge at ease
In halls well-thronged: yet, if your soul prefer,
Tarry secluded in a separate home.
Choose ye and cull, from these our proffered gifts,
Whiche'er is best and sweetest to your will:
And I and all these citizens whose vote
Stands thus decreed, will your protectors be.
Look not to find elsewhere more loyal guard.

[Footnote: 6: For this curious taunt, strongly illustrative of what Browning calls "nationality in drinks," see Herodotus, ii. 77. A similar feeling may perhaps be traced in Tacitus' description of the national beverage of the Germans: "Potui humor ex hordeo aut frumento, *in quandam similitudinem vini corruptus*" (*Germania*, chap, xxiii).]

CHORUS

O godlike chief, God grant my prayer:
Fair blessings on thy proffers fair,
Lord of Pelasgia's race!
Yet, of thy grace, unto our side
Send thou the man of courage tried,
Of counsel deep and prudent thought, —
Be Danaus to his children brought;
For his it is to guide us well
And warn where it behoves to dwell—
What place shall guard and shelter us
From malice and tongues slanderous:
Swift always are the lips of blame
A stranger-maiden to defame—
But Fortune give us grace!

THE KING OF ARGOS

A stainless fame, a welcome kind
From all this people shall ye find:
Dwell therefore, damsels, loved of us,
Within our walls, as Danaus
Allots to each, in order due,
Her dower of attendants true.
[*Re-enter* DANAUS. DANAUS

High thanks, my children, unto Argos con,
And to this folk, as to Olympian gods,
Give offerings meet of sacrifice and wine;
For saviours are they in good sooth to you.
From me they heard, and bitter was their wrath,
How those your kinsmen strove to work you wrong,
And how of us were thwarted: then to me
This company of spearmen did they grant,
That honoured I might walk, nor unaware
Die by some secret thrust and on this land
Bring down the curse of death, that dieth not.
Such boons they gave me: it behoves me pay
A deeper reverence from a soul sincere.
Ye, to the many words of wariness
Spoken by me your father, add this word,
That, tried by time, our unknown company
Be held for honest: over-swift are tongues
To slander strangers, over-light is speech
To bring pollution on a stranger's name.
Therefore I rede you, bring no shame on me
Now when man's eye beholds your maiden prime.
Lovely is beauty's ripening harvest-field,
But ill to guard; and men and beasts, I wot,
And birds and creeping things make prey of it.
And when the fruit is ripe for love, the voice
Of Aphrodite bruiteth it abroad,
The while she guards the yet unripened growth.
On the fair richness of a maiden's bloom
Each passer looks, o'ercome with strong desire,
With eyes that waft the wistful dart of love.
Then be not such our hap, whose livelong toil
Did make our pinnace plough the mighty main:
Nor bring we shame upon ourselves, and joy

Unto my foes. Behold, a twofold home—
One of the king's and one the people's gift—
Unbought, 'tis yours to hold,—a gracious boon.
Go—but remember ye your sire's behest,
And hold your life less dear than chastity.

CHORUS

The gods above grant that all else be well.
But fear not thou, O sire, lest aught befall
Of ill unto our ripened maidenhood.
So long as Heaven have no new ill devised,
From its chaste path my spirit shall not swerve.

SEMI-CHORUS

Pass and adore ye the Blessed, the gods of the city
who dwell
Around Erasinus, the gush of the swift immemorial
tide.

SEMI-CHORUS

Chant ye, O maidens; aloud let the praise of
Pelasgia swell;
Hymn we no longer the shores where Nilus to ocean
doth glide.

SEMI-CHORUS

Sing we the bounteous streams that ripple and gush
through the city;
Quickening flow they and fertile, the soft new life of
the plain.

SEMI-CHORUS

Artemis, maiden most pure, look on us with grace
and with pity—
Save us from forced embraces: such love hath no
crown but a pain.

SEMI-CHORUS

Yet not in scorn we chant, but in honour of
Aphrodite;
She truly and Hera alone have power with Zeus and
control.
Holy the deeds of her rite, her craft is secret and
mighty,
And high is her honour on earth, and subtle her
sway of the soul.

SEMI-CHORUS

Yea, and her child is Desire: in the train of his
mother he goeth—
Yea and Persuasion soft-lipped, whom none can deny
or repel:
Cometh Harmonia too, on whom Aphrodite bestoweth
The whispering parley, the paths of the rapture that
lovers love well.

SEMI-CHORUS

Ah, but I tremble and quake lest again they should
sail to reclaim!
Alas for the sorrow to come, the blood and the
carnage of war.
Ah, by whose will was it done that o'er the wide
ocean they came,
Guided by favouring winds, and wafted by sail and
by oar?

SEMI-CHORUS

Peace! for what Fate hath ordained will surely not
tarry but come;
Wide is the counsel of Zeus, by no man escaped or
withstood:
Only I Pray that whate'er, in the end, of this wedlock
he doom,
We as many a maiden of old, may win from the ill
to the good.[7]

[Footnote: 7: The ambiguity of these two lines is reproduced from the original. The Semi-Chorus appear to pray, in one aspiration, that the threatened wedlock may never take place, and, *if* it does take place, may be for weal, not woe.]

SEMI-CHORUS

Great Zeus, this wedlock turn from me—
Me from the kinsman bridegroom guard!

SEMI-CHORUS

Come what come may, 'tis Fate's decree.

SEMI-CHORUS

Soft is thy word—the doom is hard.

SEMI-CHORUS

Thou know'st not what the Fates provide.

SEMI-CHORUS

How should I scan Zeus' mighty will,
The depth of counsel undescried?

SEMI-CHORUS

Pray thou no word of omen ill.

SEMI-CHORUS

What timely warning wouldst thou teach?

SEMI-CHORUS

Beware, nor slight the gods in speech.

SEMI-CHORUS

Zeus, hold from my body the wedlock detested, the bridegroom abhorred!

It was thou, it was thou didst release
Mine ancestress Io from sorrow: thine healing it
was that restored,
The touch of thine hand gave her peace.

SEMI-CHORUS

Be thy will for the cause of the maidens! of two ills,
the lesser I pray—
The exile that leaveth me pure.
May thy justice have heed to my cause, my prayers
to thy mercy find way!
For the hands of thy saving are sure.
[*Exeunt omnes.*

THE PERSIANS

ARGUMENT

Xerxes, son of Darius and of his wife Atossa, daughter of Cyrus, went forth against Hellas, to take vengeance upon those who had defeated his father at Marathon. But ill fortune befell the king and his army both by land and sea; neither did it avail him that he cast a bridge over the Hellespont and made a canal across the promontory of Mount Athos, and brought myriads of men, by land and sea, to subdue the Greeks. For in the strait between Athens and the island of Salamis the Persian ships were shattered and sunk or put to flight by those of Athens and Lacedaemon and Aegina and Corinth, and Xerxes went homewards on the way by which he had come, leaving his general Mardonius with three hundred thousand men to strive with the Greeks by land: but in the next year they were destroyed near Plataea in Boeotia, by the Lacedaemonians and Athenians and Tegeans. Such was the end of the army which Xerxes left behind him. But the king himself had reached the bridge over the Hellespont, and late and hardly and in sorry plight and with few companions came home unto the Palace of Susa.

The Suppliant Maidens and Other Plays

DRAMATIS PERSONAE

CHORUS OF PERSIAN ELDERS.
ATOSSA, WIDOW OF DARIUS AND MOTHER OF XERXES.
A MESSENGER.
THE GHOST OF DARIUS.
XERXES.

The Scene is laid at the Palace of Susa.

CHORUS

Away unto the Grecian land
Hath passed the Persian armament:
We, by the monarch's high command,
We are the warders true who stand,
Chosen, for honour and descent,
To watch the wealth of him who went—
Guards of the gold, and faithful styled
By Xerxes, great Darius' child!

But the king went nor comes again—
And for that host, we saw depart
Arrayed in gold, my boding heart
Aches with a pulse of anxious pain,
Presageful for its youthful king!
No scout, no steed, no battle-car
Comes speeding hitherward, to bring
News to our city from afar!
Erewhile they went, away, away,
From Susa, from Ecbatana,
From Kissa's timeworn fortress grey,
Passing to ravage and to war—
Some upon steeds, on galleys some,
Some in close files, they passed from home,
All upon warlike errand bent—
Amistres, Artaphernes went,
Astaspes, Megabazes high,
Lords of the Persian chivalry,
Marshals who serve the great king's word
Chieftains of all the mighty horde!

Horsemen and bowmen streamed away,
Grim in their aspect, fixed to slay,
And resolute to face the fray!
With troops of horse, careering fast,
Masistes, Artembares passed:
Imaeus too, the bowman brave,
Sosthanes, Pharandakes, drave—
And others the all-nursing wave
Of Nilus to the battle gave;
Came Susiskanes, warrior wild,
And Pegastagon, Egypt's child:
Thee, brave Arsames! from afar
Did holy Memphis launch to war;
And Ariomardus, high in fame,
From Thebes the immemorial came,
And oarsmen skilled from Nilus' fen,
A countless crowd of warlike men:
And next, the dainty Lydians went—
Soft rulers of a continent—
Mitragathes and Arcteus bold
In twin command their ranks controlled,
And Sardis town, that teems with gold,
Sent forth its squadrons to the war—
Horse upon horse, and car on car,
Double and triple teams, they rolled,
In onset awful to behold.
From Tmolus' sacred hill there came
The native hordes to join the fray,
And upon Hellas' neck to lay
The yoke of slavery and shame;
Mardon and Tharubis were there,
Bright anvils for the foemen's spear!
The Mysian dart-men sped to war,
And the long crowd that onward rolled
From Babylon enriched with gold—
Captains of ships and archers skilled
To speed the shaft, and those who wield
The scimitar;—the eastern band
Who, by the great king's high command,
Swept to subdue the western land!

Gone are they, gone—ah, welladay!
The flower and pride of our array;
And all the Eastland, from whose breast
Came forth her bravest and her best,
Craves longingly with boding dread—
Parents for sons, and brides new-wed
For absent lords, and, day by day,
Shudder with dread at their delay!

Ere now they have passed o'er the sea,
the manifold host of the king—
They have gone forth to sack and to burn;
ashore on the Westland they spring!
With cordage and rope they have bridged
the sea-way of Helle, to pass
O'er the strait that is named by thy name,
O daughter of Athamas!
They have anchored their ships in the current,
they have bridled the neck of the sea—
The Shepherd and Lord of the East
hath bidden a roadway to be!
From the land to the land they pass over,
a herd at the high king's best;
Some by the way of the waves,
and some o'er the planking have pressed.
For the king is a lord and a god:
he was born of the golden seed
That erst upon Danae fell—
his captains are strong at the need!
And dark is the glare of his eyes,
as eyes of a serpent blood-fed,
And with manifold troops in his train
and with manifold ships hath he sped—
Yea, sped with his Syrian cars:
he leads on the lords of the bow
To meet with the men of the West,
the spear-armed force of the foe!
Can any make head and resist him,
when he comes with the roll of a wave?
No barrier nor phalanx of might,
no chief, be he ever so brave!
For stern is the onset of Persia,
and gallant her children in fight.

50

But the guile of the god is deceitful,
and who shall elude him by flight?
And who is the lord of the leap,
that can spring and alight and evade?
For Ate deludes and allures,
till round him the meshes are laid,
And no man his doom can escape!
it was writ in the rule of high Heaven,
That in tramp of the steeds and in crash of the charge
the war-cry of Persia be given:
They have learned to behold the forbidden,
the sacred enclosure of sea,
Where the waters are wide and in stress
of the wind the billows roll hoary to lee!
And their trust is in cable and cordage,
too weak in the power of the blast,
And frail are the links of the bridge
whereby unto Hellas they passed.

Therefore my gloom-wrapped heart
is rent with sorrow
For what may hap to-morrow!
Alack, for all the Persian armament—
Alack, lest there be sent
Dread news of desolation, Susa's land
Bereft, forlorn, unmanned—
Lest the grey Kissian fortress echo back
The wail, *Alack, Alack*!
The sound of women's shriek, who wail and mourn,
With fine-spun raiment torn!
The charioteers went forth nor come again,
And all the marching men
Even as a swarm of bees have flown afar,
Drawn by the king to war—
Crossing the sea-bridge, linked from side to side,
That doth the waves divide:
And the soft bridal couch of bygone years
Is now bedewed with tears,
Each princess, clad in garments delicate,
Wails for her widowed fate—

Alas my gallant bridegroom, lost and gone,
And I am left alone!

But now, ye warders of the state,
Here, in this hall of old renown,
Behoves that we deliberate
In counsel deep and wise debate,
For need is surely shown!
How fareth he, Darius' child,
The Persian king, from Perseus styled?

Comes triumph to the eastern bow,
Or hath the lance-point conquered now?
[*Enter* ATOSSA.
See, yonder comes the mother-queen,
Light of our eyes, in godlike sheen,
The royal mother of the king! —
Fall we before her! well it were
That, all as one, we sue to her,
And round her footsteps cling!

Queen, among deep-girded Persian dames thou highest and most royal,
Hoary mother, thou, of Xerxes, and Darius' wife of old!
To godlike sire, and godlike son, we bow us and are loyal—
Unless, on us, an adverse tide of destiny has rolled!

ATOSSA

Therefore come I forth to you, from chambers decked and golden,
Where long ago Darius laid his head, with me beside,
And my heart is torn with anguish, and with terror am I holden,
And I plead unto your friendship and I bid you to my side.

Darius, in the old time, by aid of some Immortal,
Raised up the stately fabric, our wealth of long-ago:
But I tremble lest it totter down, and ruin porch and portal,
And the whirling dust of downfall rise above its overthrow!

Therefore a dread unspeakable within me never slumbers, Saying,
Honour not the gauds of wealth if men have ceased to grow,
Nor deem that men, apart from wealth,
can find their strength in numbers—
We shudder for our light and king, though we have gold enow!

No light there is, in any house, save presence of the master—
So runs the saw, ye aged men! and truth it says indeed—
On you I call, the wise and true, to ward us from disaster,
For all my hope is fixed on you, to prop us in our need!

CHORUS

Queen-Mother of the Persian land, to thy commandment bowing,
Whate'er thou wilt, in word or deed, we follow to fulfil—
Not twice we need thine high behest, our faith and duty knowing,
In council and in act alike, thy loyal servants still!

ATOSSA

Long while by various visions of the night
Am I beset, since to Ionian lands
With marshalled host my son went forth to war.
Yet never saw I presage so distinct
As in the night now passed.—Attend my tale!—
A dream I had: two women nobly clad
Came to my sight, one robed in Persian dress,
The other vested in the Dorian garb,
And both right stately and more tall by far
Than women of to-day, and beautiful
Beyond disparagement, and sisters sprung

Both of one race, but, by their natal lot,
One born in Hellas, one in Eastern land.
These, as it seemed unto my watching eyes,
Roused each the other to a mutual feud:
The which my son perceiving set himself
To check and soothe their struggle, and anon
Yoked them and set the collars on their necks;
And one, the Ionian, proud in this array,
Paced in high quietude, and lent her mouth,
Obedient, to the guidance of the rein.
But restively the other strove, and broke
The fittings of the car, and plunged away
With mouth un-bitted: o'er the broken yoke
My son was hurled, and lo! Darius stood
In lamentation o'er his fallen child.
Him Xerxes saw, and rent his robe in grief.

Such was my vision of the night now past;
But when, arising, I had dipped my hand
In the fair lustral stream, I drew towards
The altar, in the act of sacrifice,
Having in mind to offer, as their due,
The sacred meal-cake to the averting powers,
Lords of the rite that banisheth ill dreams.
When lo! I saw an eagle fleeing fast
To Phoebus' shrine—O friends, I stayed my steps,
Too scared to speak! for, close upon his flight,
A little falcon dashed in winged pursuit,
Plucking with claws the eagle's head, while he
Could only crouch and cower and yield himself.
Scared was I by that sight, and eke to you
No less a terror must it be to hear!
For mark this well—if Xerxes have prevailed,
He shall come back the wonder of the world:
If not, still none can call him to account—
So he but live, he liveth Persia's King!

CHORUS

Queen, it stands not with my purpose to abet these fears of thine,
Nor to speak with glazing comfort! nay, betake thee to the shrine!
If thy dream foretold disaster, sue to gods to bar its way,
And, for thyself, son, state, and friends, to bring fair fate
to-day.
Next, unto Earth and to the Dead be due libation poured,
And by thee let Darius' soul be wistfully implored—
I saw thee, lord, in last night's dream, a phantom from the grave,
I pray thee, lord, from earth beneath come forth to help and save!
To me and to thy son send up the bliss of triumph now,
And hold the gloomy fates of ill, dim in the dark below!
Such be thy words! my inner heart good tidings doth foretell,
And that fair fate will spring thereof, if wisdom guide us well.

ATOSSA

Loyal thou that first hast read this dream, this vision of the
night,
With loyalty to me, the queen—be then thy presage right!
And therefore, as thy bidding is, what time I pass within
To dedicate these offerings, new prayers I will begin,
Alike to gods and the great dead who loved our lineage well.
Yet one more word—say, in what realm do the Athenians dwell?

CHORUS

Far hence, even where, in evening land, goes down our Lord the
Sun.

ATOSSA

Say, had my son so keen desire, that region to o'errun?

CHORUS

Yea—if she fell, the rest of Greece were subject to our sway!

ATOSSA

Hath she so great predominance, such legions in array?

CHORUS

Ay—such a host as smote us sore upon an earlier day.

ATOSSA

And what hath she, besides her men? enow of wealth in store?

CHORUS

A mine of treasure in the earth, a fount of silver ore!

ATOSSA

Is it in skill of bow and shaft that Athens' men excel?

CHORUS

Nay, they bear bucklers in the fight,
and thrust the spear-point well.

ATOSSA

And who is shepherd of their host and holds them in command?

CHORUS

To no man do they bow as slaves, nor own a master's hand.

ATOSSA

How should they bide our brunt of war, the East upon the West?

CHORUS

That could Darius' valiant horde in days of yore attest!

ATOSSA

A boding word, to us who bore the men now far away!

CHORUS

Nay—as I deem, the very truth will dawn on us to-day.
A Persian by his garb and speed, a courier draws anear—
He bringeth news, of good or ill, for Persia's land to hear.
[*Enter* A MESSENGER.
MESSENGER

O walls and towers of all the Asian realm,
O Persian land, O treasure-house of gold!
How, by one stroke, down to destruction, down,
Hath sunk our pride, and all the flower of war
That once was Persia's, lieth in the dust!
Woe on the man who first announceth woe—
Yet must I all the tale of death unroll!
Hark to me, Persians! Persia's host lies low.

CHORUS

O ruin manifold, and woe, and fear!
Let the wild tears run down, for the great doom is here!

MESSENGER

This blow hath fallen, to the utterance, And I, past hope, behold
my safe return!

CHORUS

Too long, alack, too long this life of mine,
That in mine age I see this sudden woe condign!

MESSENGER

As one who saw, by no loose rumour led,
Lords, I would tell what doom was dealt to us.

CHORUS

Alack, how vainly have they striven!
Our myriad hordes with shaft and bow
Went from the Eastland, to lay low
Hellas, beloved of Heaven!

MESSENGER

Piled with men dead, yea, miserably slain,
Is every beach, each reef of Salamis!

CHORUS

Thou sayest sooth—ah well-a-day!
Battered amid the waves, and torn,
On surges hither, thither, borne,
Dead bodies, bloodstained and forlorn,
In their long cloaks they toss and stray!

MESSENGER

Their bows availed not! all have perished, all,
By charging galleys crushed and whelmed in death.

CHORUS

Shriek out your sorrow's wistful wail!
To their untimely doom they went;
Ill strove they, and to no avail,
And minished is their armament!

MESSENGER

Out on thee, hateful name of Salamis,
Out upon Athens, mournful memory!

CHORUS

Woe upon this day's evil fame!
Thou, Athens, art our murderess;
Alack, full many a Persian dame
Is left forlorn and husbandless!

ATOSSA

Mute have I been awhile, and overwrought
At this great sorrow, for it passeth speech,
And passeth all desire to ask of it.
Yet if the gods send evils, men must bear.
(*To the* MESSENGER)
Unroll the record! stand composed and tell,
Although thy heart be groaning inwardly,
Who hath escaped, and, of our leaders, whom
Have we to weep? what chieftains in the van
Stood, sank, and died and left us leaderless?

MESSENGER

Xerxes himself survives and sees the day.

ATOSSA

Then to my line thy word renews the dawn
And golden dayspring after gloom of night!

MESSENGER

But the brave marshal of ten thousand horse,
Artembares, is tossed and flung in death
Along the rugged rocks Silenian.
And Dadaces no longer leads his troop,
But, smitten by the spear, from off the prow
Hath lightly leaped to death; and Tenagon,
In true descent a Bactrian nobly born,
Drifts by the sea-lashed reefs of Salamis,
The isle of Ajax. Gone Lilaeus too,
Gone are Arsames and Argestes! all,
Around the islet where the sea-doves breed,
Dashed their defeated heads on iron rocks;
Arcteus, who dwelt beside the founts of Nile,
Adeues, Pheresseues, and with them
Pharnuchus, from one galley's deck went down.
Matallus, too, of Chrysa, lord and king
Of myriad hordes, who led unto the fight
Three times ten thousand swarthy cavaliers,
Fell, with his swarthy and abundant beard

Incarnadined to red, a crimson stain
Outrivalling the purple of the sea!
There Magian Arabus and Artames
Of Bactra perished—taking up, alike,
In yonder stony land their long sojourn.
Amistris too, and he whose strenuous spear
Was foremost in the fight, Amphistreus fell,
And gallant Ariomardus, by whose death
Broods sorrow upon Sardis: Mysia mourns
For Seisames, and Tharubis lies low—
Commander, he, of five times fifty ships,
Born in Lyrnessus: his heroic form
Is low in death, ungraced with sepulchre.
Dead too is he, the lord of courage high,
Cilicia's marshal, brave Syennesis,
Than whom none dealt more carnage on the foe,
Nor perished by a more heroic end.
So fell the brave: so speak I of their doom,
Summing in brief the fate of myriads!

ATOSSA

Ah well-a-day! these crowning woes I hear,
The shame of Persia and her shrieks of dole!
But yet renew the tale, repeat thy words,
Tell o'er the count of those Hellenic ships,
And how they ventured with their beaked prows
To charge upon the Persian armament.

MESSENGER

Know, if mere count of ships could win the day,
The Persians had prevailed. The Greeks, in sooth,
Had but three hundred galleys at the most,
And other ten, select and separate.
But—I am witness—Xerxes held command
Of full a thousand keels, and, those apart,
Two hundred more, and seven, for speed renowned!—
So stands the reckoning, and who shall dare
To say we Persians had the lesser host?

ATOSSA

Nay, we were worsted by an unseen power
Who swayed the balance downward to our doom!

MESSENGER

In ward of heaven doth Pallas' city stand.

ATOSSA

How then? is Athens yet inviolate?

MESSENGER

While her men live, her bulwark standeth firm!

ATOSSA

Say, how began the struggle of the ships?
Who first joined issue? did the Greeks attack,
Or Xerxes, in his numbers confident?

MESSENGER

O queen, our whole disaster thus befell,
Through intervention of some fiend or fate—
I know not what—that had ill will to us.
From the Athenian host some Greek came o'er,
To thy son Xerxes whispering this tale—
Once let the gloom of night have gathered in,
The Greeks will tarry not, but swiftly spring
Each to his galley-bench, in furtive flight,
Softly contriving safety for their life.
Thy son believed the word and missed the craft
Of that Greek foeman, and the spite of Heaven,
And straight to all his captains gave this charge—
As soon as sunlight warms the ground no more,
And gloom enwraps the sanctuary of sky,
Range we our fleet in triple serried lines
To bar the passage from the seething strait,
This way and that: let other ships surround
The isle of Ajax, with this warning word—

That if the Greeks their jeopardy should scape
By wary craft, and win their ships a road.
Each Persian captain shall his failure pay
By forfeit of his head. So spake the king,
Inspired at heart with over-confidence,
Unwitting of the gods' predestined will.
Thereon our crews, with no disordered haste,
Did service to his bidding and purveyed
The meal of afternoon: each rower then
Over the fitted rowlock looped his oar.
Then, when the splendour of the sun had set,
And night drew on, each master of the oar
And each armed warrior straightway went aboard.
Forward the long ships moved, rank cheering rank,
Each forward set upon its ordered course.
And all night long the captains of the fleet
Kept their crews moving up and down the strait.
So the night waned, and not one Grecian ship
Made effort to elude and slip away.
But as dawn came and with her coursers white
Shone in fair radiance over all the earth,
First from the Grecian fleet rang out a cry,
A song of onset! and the island crags
Re-echoed to the shrill exulting sound.
Then on us Eastern men amazement fell
And fear in place of hope; for what we heard
Was not a call to flight! the Greeks rang out
Their holy, resolute, exulting chant,
Like men come forth to dare and do and die
Their trumpets pealed, and fire was in that sound,
And with the dash of simultaneous oars
Replying to the war-chant, on they came,
Smiting the swirling brine, and in a trice
They flashed upon the vision of the foe!
The right wing first in orderly advance
Came on, a steady column; following then,
The rest of their array moved out and on,
And to our ears there came a burst of sound,
A clamour manifold. — *On, sons of Greece!*
On, for your country's freedom! strike to save
Wives, children, temples of ancestral gods,
Graves of your fathers! now is all at stake.
Then from our side swelled up the mingled din

Of Persian tongues, and time brooked no delay —
Ship into ship drave hard its brazen beak
With speed of thought, a shattering blow! and first
One Grecian bark plunged straight, and sheared away
Bowsprit and stem of a Phoenician ship.
And then each galley on some other's prow
Came crashing in. Awhile our stream of ships
Held onward, till within the narrowing creek
Our jostling vessels were together driven,
And none could aid another: each on each
Drave hard their brazen beaks, or brake away
The oar-banks of each other, stem to stern,
While the Greek galleys, with no lack of skill,
Hemmed them and battered in their sides, and soon
The hulls rolled over, and the sea was hid,
Crowded with wrecks and butchery of men.
No beach nor reef but was with corpses strewn,
And every keel of our barbarian host
Hurried to flee, in utter disarray.
Thereon the foe closed in upon the wrecks
And hacked and hewed, with oars and splintered planks,
As fishermen hack tunnies or a cast
Of netted dolphins, and the briny sea
Rang with the screams and shrieks of dying men,
Until the night's dark aspect hid the scene.
Had I a ten days' time to sum that count
Of carnage, 'twere too little! know this well —
One day ne'er saw such myriad forms of death!

ATOSSA

Woe on us, woe! disaster's mighty sea
Hath burst on us and all the Persian realm!

MESSENGER

Be well assured, the tale is but begun —
The further agony that on us fell
Doth twice outweigh the sufferings I have told!

ATOSSA

Nay, what disaster could be worse than this?
Say on! what woe upon the army came,
Swaying the scale to a yet further fall?

MESSENGER

The very flower and crown of Persia's race,
Gallant of soul and glorious in descent,
And highest held in trust before the king,
Lies shamefully and miserably slain.

ATOSSA

Alas for me and for this ruin, friends!
Dead, sayest thou? by what fate overthrown?

MESSENGER

An islet is there, fronting Salamis—
Strait, and with evil anchorage: thereon
Pan treads the measure of the dance he loves
Along the sea-beach. Thither the king sent
His noblest, that, whene'er the Grecian foe
Should 'scape, with shattered ships, unto the isle,
We might make easy prey of fugitives
And slay them there, and from the washing tides
Rescue our friends. It fell out otherwise
Than he divined, for when, by aid of Heaven,
The Hellenes held the victory on the sea,
Their sailors then and there begirt themselves
With brazen mail and bounded from their ships,
And then enringed the islet, point by point,
So that our Persians in bewilderment
Knew not which way to turn. On every side,
Battered with stones, they fell, while arrows flew
From many a string, and smote them to the death.
Then, at the last, with simultaneous rush
The foe came bursting on us, hacked and hewed
To fragments all that miserable band,
Till not a soul of them was left alive.
Then Xerxes saw disaster's depth, and shrieked,

64

From where he sat on high, surveying all —
A lofty eminence, beside the brine,
Whence all his armament lay clear in view.
His robe he rent, with loud and bitter wail,
And to his land-force swiftly gave command
And fled, with shame beside him! Now, lament
That second woe, upon the first imposed!

ATOSSA

Out on thee, Fortune! thou hast foiled the hope
And power of Persia: to this bitter end
My son went forth to wreak his great revenge
On famous Athens! all too few they seemed,
Our men who died upon the Fennel-field!
Vengeance for them my son had mind to take,
And drew on his own head these whelming woes.
But thou, say on! the ships that 'scaped from wreck —
Where didst thou leave them? make thy story clear.

MESSENGER

The captains of the ships that still survived
Fled in disorder, scudding down the wind,
The while our land-force on Boeotian soil
Fell into ruin, some beside the springs
Dropping before they drank, and some outworn,
Pursued, and panting all their life away.
The rest of us our way to Phocis won,
And thence to Doris and the Melian gulf,
Where with soft stream Spercheus laves the soil.
Thence to the northward did Phthiotis' plain,
And some Thessalian fortress, lend us aid,
For famine-pinched we were, and many died
Of drought and hunger's twofold present scourge.
Thence to Magnesia came we, and the land
Where Macedonians dwell, and crossed the ford
Of Axius, and Bolbe's reedy fen,
And mount Pangaeus, in Edonian land.
There, in the very night we came, the god
Brought winter ere its time, from bank to bank
Freezing the holy Strymon's tide. Each man
Who heretofore held lightly of the gods,

Now crouched and proffered prayer to Earth and Heaven!
Then, after many orisons performed,
The army ventured on the frozen ford:
Yet only those who crossed before the sun
Shed its warm rays, won to the farther side.
For soon the fervour of the glowing orb
Did with its keen rays pierce the ice-bound stream,
And men sank through and thrust each other down—
Best was his lot whose breath was stifled first!
But all who struggled through and gained the bank,
Toilfully wending through the land of Thrace
Have made their way, a sorry, scanted few,
Unto this homeland. Let the city now
Lament and yearn for all the loved and lost.
My tale is truth, yet much untold remains
Of ills that Heaven hath hurled upon our land.

CHORUS

Spirit of Fate, too heavy were thy feet,
Those ill to match! that sprang on Persia's realm.

ATOSSA

Woe for the host, to wrack and ruin hurled!
O warning of the night, prophetic dream!
Thou didst foreshadow clearly all the doom,
While ye, old men, made light of woman's fears!
Ah well—yet, as your divination ruled
The meaning of the sign, I hold it good,
First, that I put up prayer unto the gods,
And, after that, forth from my palace bring
The sacrificial cake, the offering due
To Earth and to the spirits of the dead.
Too well I know it is a timeless rite
Over a finished thing that cannot change!
But yet—I know not—there may come of it
Alleviation for the after time.
You it beseems, in view of what hath happed,
T' advise with loyal hearts our loyal guards:
And to my son—if, ere my coming forth,
He should draw hitherward—give comfort meet,
Escort him to the palace in all state,

66

Lest to these woes he add another woe!
[*Exit* ATOSSA.

CHORUS

Zeus, lord and king! to death and nought
Our countless host by thee is brought.
Deep in the gloom of death, to-day,
Lie Susa and Ecbatana:
How many a maid in sorrow stands
And rends her tire with tender hands!
How tears run down, in common pain
And woeful mourning for the slain!
O delicate in dole and grief,
Ye Persian women! past relief
Is now your sorrow! to the war
Your loved ones went and come no more!
Gone from you is your joy and pride—
Severed the bridegroom from the bride—
The wedded couch luxurious
Is widowed now, and all the house
Pines ever with insatiate sighs,
And we stand here and bid arise,
For those who forth in ardour went
And come not back, the loud lament!

Land of the East, thou mournest for the host,
Bereft of all thy sons, alas the day!
For them whom Xerxes led hath Xerxes lost—
Xerxes who wrecked the fleet, and flung our hopes away!

How came it that Darius once controlled,
And without scathe, the army of the bow,
Loved by the folk of Susa, wise and bold?
Now is the land-force lost, the shipmen sunk below!

Ah for the ships that bore them, woe is me!
Bore them to death and doom! the crashing prows
Of fierce Ionian oarsmen swept the sea,
And death was in their wake, and shipwreck murderous!

Late, late and hardly—if true tales they tell—
Did Xerxes flee along the wintry way

And snows of Thrace—but ah, the first who fell
Lie by the rocks or float upon Cychrea's bay!

Mourn, each and all! waft heavenward your cry,
Stung to the soul, bereaved, disconsolate!
Wail out your anguish, till it pierce the sky,
In shrieks of deep despair, ill-omened, desperate!

The dead are drifting, yea, are gnawed upon
By voiceless children of the stainless sea,
Or battered by the surge! we mourn and groan
For husbands gone to death, for childless agony!

Alas the aged men, who mourn to-day
The ruinous sorrows that the gods ordain!
O'er the wide Asian land, the Persian sway
Can force no tribute now, and can no rule sustain.

Yea, men will crouch no more to fallen power
And kingship overthrown! the whole land o'er,
Men speak the thing they will, and from this hour
The folk whom Xerxes ruled obey his word no more.

The yoke of force is broken from the neck—
The isle of Ajax and th' encircling wave
Reek with a bloody crop of death and wreck
Of Persia's fallen power, that none can lift nor save!
[Re-enter ATOSSA, in mourning robes.

ATOSSA

Friends, whosoe'er is versed in human ills,
Knoweth right well that when a wave of woe
Comes on a man, he sees in all things fear;
While, in flood-tide of fortune, 'tis his mood
To take that fortune as unchangeable,
Wafting him ever forward. Mark me now—
The gods' thwart purpose doth confront mine eyes,
And all is terror to me; in mine ears
There sounds a cry, but not of triumph now—
So am I scared at heart by woe so great.
Therefore I wend forth from the house anew,
Borne in no car of state, nor robed in pride

68

As heretofore, but bringing, for the sire
Who did beget my son, libations meet
For holy rites that shall appease the dead —
The sweet white milk, drawn from a spotless cow,
The oozing drop of golden honey, culled
By the flower-haunting bee, and therewithal
Pure draughts of water from a virgin spring;
And lo! besides, the stainless effluence,
Born of the wild vine's bosom, shining store
Treasured to age, this bright and luscious wine.
And eke the fragrant fruit upon the bough
Of the grey olive-tree, which lives its life
In sprouting leafage, and the twining flowers,
Bright children of the earth's fertility.
But you, O friends! above these offerings poured
To reconcile the dead, ring out your dirge
To summon up Darius from the shades,
Himself a shade; and I will pour these draughts,
Which earth shall drink, unto the gods of hell.

CHORUS

Queen, by the Persian land adored,
By thee be this libation poured,
Passing to those who hold command
Of dead men in the spirit-land!
And we will sue, in solemn chant,
That gods who do escort the dead
In nether realms, our prayer may grant —
Back to us be Darius led!

O Earth, and Hermes, and the king
Of Hades, our Darius bring!
For if, beyond the prayers we prayed,
He knoweth aught of help or aid,
He, he alone, in realms below,
Can speak the limit of our woe!

Doth he hear me, the king we adored, who is god
among gods of the dead?
Doth he hear me send out in my sorrow the pitiful,
manifold cry,
The sobbing lament and appeal? is the voice of my

suffering sped
To the realm of the shades? doth he hear me and
pity my sorrowful sigh?
O Earth, and ye Lords of the dead! release ye that
spirit of might,
Who in Susa the palace was born! let him rise up
once more to the light!

There is none like him, none of all
That e'er were laid in Persian sepulchres!
Borne forth he was to honoured burial,
A royal heart! and followed by our tears.
God of the dead, O give him back to us,
Darius, ruler glorious!
He never wasted us with reckless war—
God, counsellor, and king, beneath a happy star!
Ancient of days and king, awake and come—
Rise o'er the mounded tomb!
Rise, plant thy foot, with saffron sandal shod
Father to us, and god!
Rise with thy diadem, O sire benign,
Upon thy brow!
List to the strange new sorrows of thy line,
Sire of a woeful son!

A mist of fate and hell is round us now,
And all the city's flower to death is done!
Alas, we wept thee once, and weep again!
O Lord of lords, by recklessness twofold
The land is wasted of its men,
And down to death are rolled
Wreckage of sail and oar,
Ships that are ships no more,
And bodies of the slain!
[The GHOST OF DARIUS rises.

GHOST OF DARIUS

Ye aged Persians, truest of the true,
Coevals of the youth that once was mine,
What troubleth now our city? harken, how
It moans and beats the breast and rends the plain!
And I, beholding how my consort stood
Beside my tomb, was moved with awe, and took
The gift of her libation graciously.
But ye are weeping by my sepulchre,
And, shrilling forth a sad, evoking cry,
Summon me mournfully, *Arise, arise.*
No light thing is it, to come back from death,
For, in good sooth, the gods of nether gloom
Are quick to seize but late and loth to free!
Yet among them I dwell as one in power—
And lo, I come! now speak, and speed your words,
Lest I be blamed for tarrying overlong!
What new disaster broods o'er Persia's realm?

CHORUS

With awe on thee I gaze,
And, standing face to face,
I tremble as I did in olden days!

GHOST OF DARIUS

Nay, but as I rose to earth again, obedient to your call,
Prithee, tarry not in parley! be one word enough for all—
Speak and gaze on me unshrinking, neither let my face appal!

CHORUS

I tremble to reveal,
Yet tremble to conceal
Things hard for friends to feel!

GHOST OF DARIUS

Nay, but if the old-time terror on your spirit keeps its hold,
Speak thou, O royal lady who didst couch with me of old!
Stay thy weeping and lamenting and to me reveal the truth—
Speak! for man is born to sorrow; yea, the proverb sayeth sooth!
'Tis the doom of mortal beings, if they live to see old age,
To suffer bale, by land and sea, through war and tempest's rage.

ATOSSA

O thou whose blissful fate on earth all mortal weal excelled—
Who, while the sunlight touched thine eyes, the lord of all wert held!
A god to Persian men thou wert, in bliss and pride and fame—
I hold thee blest too in thy death, or e'er the ruin came!
Alas, Darius! one brief word must tell thee all the tale—
The Persian power is in the dust, gone down in blood and bale!

GHOST OF DARIUS

Speak—by what chance? did man rebel, or pestilence descend?

ATOSSA

Neither! by Athens' fatal shores our army met its end.

GHOST OF DARIUS

Which of my children led our host to Athens? speak and say.

ATOSSA

The froward Xerxes, leaving all our realm to disarray.

GHOST OF DARIUS

Was it with army or with fleet on folly's quest he went?

ATOSSA

With both alike, a twofold front of double armament.

GHOST OF DARIUS

And how then did so large a host on foot pass o'er the sea?

ATOSSA

He bridged the ford of Helle's strait by artful carpentry.

GHOST OF DARIUS

How? could his craft avail to span the torrent of that tide?

ATOSSA

'Tis sooth I say—some unknown power did fatal help provide!

GHOST OF DARIUS

Alas, that power in malice came, to his bewilderment!

ATOSSA

Alas, we see the end of all, the ruin on us sent.

GHOST OF DARIUS

Speak, tell me how they fared therein, that thus ye mourn and weep?

ATOSSA

Disaster to the army came, through ruin on the deep!

GHOST OF DARIUS

Is all undone? hath all the folk gone down before the foe?

ATOSSA

Yea, hark to Susa's mourning cry for warriors laid low!

GHOST OF DARIUS

Alas for all our gallant aids, our Persia's help and pride!

ATOSSA

Ay! old with young, the Bactrian force hath perished at our side!

GHOST OF DARIUS

Alas, my son! what gallant youths hath he sent down to death!

ATOSSA

Alone, or with a scanty guard—for so the rumour saith—

GHOST OF DARIUS

He came—but how, and to what end? doth aught of hope remain?

ATOSSA

With joy he reached the bridge that spanned the Hellespontine main.

GHOST OF DARIUS

How? is he safe, in Persian land? speak soothly, yea or nay!

ATOSSA

Clear and more clear the rumour comes, for no man to gainsay.

GHOST OF DARIUS

Woe for the oracle fulfilled, the presage of the war
Launched on my son, by will of Zeus! I deemed our doom afar
In lap of time; but, if a king push forward to his fate,
The god himself allures to death that man infatuate!
So now the very fount of woe streams out on those I loved,
And mine own son, unwisely bold, the truth hereof hath proved!
He sought to shackle and control the Hellespontine wave,
That rushes from the Bosphorus, with fetters of a slave!—
To curb and bridge, with welded links, the streaming water-way,
And guide across the passage broad his manifold array!
Ah, folly void of counsel! he deemed that mortal wight
Could thwart the will of Heaven itself and curb Poseidon's might!
Was it not madness? much I fear lest all my wealth and store

Pass from my treasure-house, to be the snatcher's prize once more!

ATOSSA

Such is the lesson, ah, too late! to eager Xerxes taught—
Trusting random counsellors and hare-brained men of nought,
Who said *Darius mighty wealth and fame to us did bring,*
But thou art nought, a blunted spear, a palace-keeping king!
Unto those sorry counsellors a ready ear he lent,
And led away to Hellas' shore his fated armament.

GHOST OF DARIUS

Therefore through them hath come calamity
Most huge and past forgetting; nor of old
Did ever such extermination fall
Upon the city Susa. Long ago
Zeus in his power this privilege bestowed,
That with a guiding sceptre one sole man
Should rule this Asian land of flock and herd.
Over the folk a Mede, Astyages,
Did grasp the power: then Cyaxares ruled
In his sire's place, and held the sway aright,
Steering his state with watchful wariness.
Third in succession, Cyrus, blest of Heaven,
Held rule and 'stablished peace for all his clan:
Lydian and Phrygian won he to his sway,
And wide Ionia to his yoke constrained,
For the god favoured his discretion sage.
Fourth in the dynasty was Cyrus' son,
And fifth was Mardus, scandal of his land
And ancient lineage. Him Artaphrenes,
Hardy of heart, within his palace slew,
Aided by loyal plotters, set for this.
And I too gained the lot for which I craved,
And oftentimes led out a goodly host,
Yet never brought disaster such as this
Upon the city. But my son is young
And reckless in his youth, and heedeth not
The warnings of my mouth. Mark this, my friends,
Born with my birth, coeval with mine age—
Not all we kings who held successive rule
Have wrought, combined, such ruin as my son!

75

CHORUS

How then, O King Darius? whitherward
Dost thou direct thy warning? from this plight
How can we Persians fare towards hope again?

GHOST OF DARIUS

By nevermore assailing Grecian lands,
Even tho' our Median force be double theirs—
For the land's self protects its denizens.

CHORUS

How meanest thou? by what defensive power?

GHOST OF DARIUS

She wastes by famine a too countless foe.

CHORUS

But we will bring a host more skilled than huge.

GHOST OF DARIUS

Why, e'en that army, camped in Hellas still,
Shall never win again to home and weal!

CHORUS

How say'st thou? will not all the Asian host
Pass back from Europe over Helle's ford?

GHOST OF DARIUS

Nay—scarce a tithe of all those myriads,
If man may trust the oracles of Heaven
When he beholds the things already wrought,
Not false with true, but true with no word false
If what I trow be truth, my son has left
A chosen rear-guard of our host, in whom
He trusts, now, with a random confidence!
They tarry where Asopus laves the ground
With rills that softly bless Boeotia's plain—
There is it fated for them to endure
The very crown of misery and doom,
Requital for their god-forgetting pride!
For why? they raided Hellas, had the heart
To wrong the images of holy gods,
And give the shrines and temples to the flame!
Defaced and dashed from sight the altars fell,
And each god's image, from its pedestal
Thrust and flung down, in dim confusion lies!
Therefore, for outrage vile, a doom as dark
They suffer, and yet more shall undergo—
They touch no bottom in the swamp of doom,
But round them rises, bubbling up, the ooze!
So deep shall lie the gory clotted mass
Of corpses by the Dorian spear transfixed
Upon Plataea's field! yea, piles of slain
To the third generation shall attest
By silent eloquence to those that see—
Let not a mortal vaunt him overmuch.
For pride grows rankly, and to ripeness brings
The curse of fate, and reaps, for harvest, tears!
Therefore when ye behold, for deeds like these,
Such stern requital paid, remember then
Athens and Hellas. Let no mortal wight,
Holding too lightly of his present weal
And passionate for more, cast down and spill
The mighty cup of his prosperity!
Doubt not that over-proud and haughty souls
Zeus lours in wrath, exacting the account.
Therefore, with wary warning, school my son,
Though he be lessoned by the gods already,
To curb the vaunting that affronts high Heaven!

77

And thou, O venerable Mother-queen,
Beloved of Xerxes, to the palace pass
And take therefrom such raiment as befits
Thy son, and go to meet him: for his garb
In this extremity of grief hangs rent
Around his body, woefully unstitched,
Mere tattered fragments of once royal robes!
Go thou to him, speak soft and soothing words —
Thee, and none other, will he bear to hear,
As well I know. But I must pass away
From earth above, unto the nether gloom;
Therefore, old men, take my farewell, and clasp,
Even amid the ruin of this time,
Unto your souls the pleasure of the day,
For dead men have no profit of their gold!
[*The* GHOST OF DARIUS *sinks.*

CHORUS

Alas, I thrill with pain for Persia's woes —
Many fulfilled, and others hard at hand!

ATOSSA

O spirit of the race, what sorrows crowd
Upon me! and this anguish stings me worst,
That round my royal son's dishonoured form
Hang rags and tatters, degradation deep!
I will away, and, bringing from within
A seemly royal robe, will straightway strive
To meet and greet my son: foul scorn it were
To leave our dearest in his hour of shame.
[*Exit* ATOSSA.

CHORUS

Ah glorious and goodly they were,
the life and the lot that we gained,
The cities we held in our hand
when the monarch invincible reigned,
The king that was good to his realm,
sufficing, fulfilled of his sway,
A lord that was peer of the gods,
the pride of the bygone day!
Then could we show to the skies
great hosts and a glorious name,
And laws that were stable in might;
as towers they guarded our fame!
There without woe or disaster
we came from the foe and the fight,
In triumph, enriched with the spoil,
to the land and the city's delight.
What towns ere the Halys he passed!
what towns ere he came to the West,
To the main and the isles of the Strymon,
and the Thracian region possess'd!
And those that stand back from the main,
enringed by their fortified wall,
Gave o'er to Darius, the king,
the sceptre and sway over all!
Those too by the channel of Helle,
where southward it broadens and glides,
By the inlets, Propontis! of thee,
and the strait of the Pontic tides,
And the isles that lie fronting our sea-board,
and the Eastland looks on each one,
Lesbo and Chios and Paros,
and Samos with olive-trees grown,
And Naxos, and Myconos' rock,
and Tenos with Andros hard by,
And isles that in midmost Aegean,
aloof from the continent, lie —
And Lemnos and Icaros' hold —
all these to his sceptre were bowed,
And Cnidos and neighbouring Rhodes,
and Soli, and Paphos the proud,
And Cyprian Salamis, name-child of her

who hath wrought us this wrong!
Yea, and all the Ionian tract,
where the Greek-born inhabitants throng,
And the cities are teeming with gold—
Darius was lord of them all,
And, great by his wisdom, he ruled,
and ever there came to his call,
In stalwart array and unfailing,
the warrior chiefs of our land,
And mingled allies from the tribes
who bowed to his conquering hand!
But now there are none to gainsay
that the gods are against us; we lie
Subdued in the havoc of wreck,
and whelmed by the wrath of the sky!
[*Enter* XERXES *in disarray.*

XERXES

Alas the day, that I should fall
Into this grimmest fate of all,
This ruin doubly unforeseen!
On Persia's land what power of Fate
Descends, what louring gloom of hate?
How shall I bear my teen?
My limbs are loosened where they stand,
When I behold this aged band—
Oh God! I would that I too, I,
Among the men who went to die,
Were whelmed in earth by Fate's command!

CHORUS

Ah welladay, my King! ah woe
For all our heroes' overthrow—
For all the gallant host's array,
For Persia's honour, pass'd away,
For glory and heroic sway
Mown down by Fortune's hand to-day!
Hark, how the kingdom makes its moan,
For youthful valour lost and gone,
By Xerxes shattered and undone!
He, he hath crammed the maw of hell

With bowmen brave, who nobly fell,
Their country's mighty armament,
Ten thousand heroes deathward sent!
Alas, for all the valiant band,
O king and lord! thine Asian land
Down, down upon its knee is bent!

XERXES

Alas, a lamentable sound,
A cry of ruth! for I am found
A curse to land and lineage,
With none my sorrow to assuage!

CHORUS

Alas, a death-song desolate
I send forth, for thy home-coming!
A scream, a dirge for woe and fate,
Such as the Asian mourners sing,
A sorry and ill-omened tale
Of tears and shrieks and Eastern wail!

XERXES

Ay, launch the woeful sorrow's cry,
The harsh, discordant melody,
For lo, the power, we held for sure,
Hath turned to my discomfiture!

CHORUS

Yea, dirges, dirges manifold
Will I send forth, for warriors bold,
For the sea-sorrow of our host!
The city mourns, and I must wail
With plashing tears our sorrow's tale,
Lamenting for the loved and lost!

XERXES

Alas, the god of war, who sways
The scales of fight in diverse ways,
Gives glory to Ionia!
Ionian ships, in fenced array,
Have reaped their harvest in the bay,
A darkling harvest-field of Fate,
A sea, a shore, of doom and hate!

CHORUS

Cry out, and learn the tale of woe!
Where are thy comrades? where the band
Who stood beside thee, hand in hand,
A little while ago?
Where now hath Pharandakes gone,
Where Psammis, and where Pelagon?
Where now is brave Agdabatas,
And Susas too, and Datamas?
Hath Susiscanes past away,
The chieftain of Ecbatana?

XERXES

I left them, mangled castaways,
Flung from their Tyrian deck, and tossed
On Salaminian water-ways,
From surging tides to rocky coast!

CHORUS

Alack, and is Pharnuchus slain,
And Ariomardus, brave in vain?
Where is Seualces' heart of fire?
Lilaeus, child of noble sire?
Are Tharubis and Memphis sped?
Hystaechmas, Artembares dead?
And where is brave Masistes, where?
Sum up death's count, that I may hear!

XERXES

Alas, alas, they came, their eyes surveyed
Ancestral Athens on that fatal day.
Then with a rending struggle were they laid
Upon the land, and gasped their life away!

CHORUS

And Batanochus' child, Alpistus great,
Surnamed the Eye of State—
Saw you and left you him who once of old
Ten thousand thousand fighting-men enrolled?
His sire was child of Sesamas, and he
From Megabates sprang. Ah, woe is me,
Thou king of evil fate!
Hast thou lost Parthus, lost Oebares great?
Alas, the sorrow! blow succeedeth blow
On Persia's pride; thou tellest woe on woe!

XERXES

Bitter indeed the pang for comrades slain,
The brave and bold! thou strikest to my soul
Pain, pain beyond forgetting, hateful pain.
My inner spirit sobs and sighs with dole!

CHORUS

Another yet we yearn to see,
And see not! ah, thy chivalry,
Xanthis, thou chief of Mardian men
Countless! and thou, Anchares bright,
And ye, whose cars controlled the fight,
Arsaces and Diaixis wight,
Kegdadatas, Lythimnas dear,
And Tolmus, greedy of the spear!
I stand bereft! not in thy train
Come they, as erst! ah, ne'er again
Shall they return unto our eyes,
Car-borne, 'neath silken canopies!

XERXES

Yea, gone are they who mustered once the host!

CHORUS

Yea, yea, forgotten, lost!

XERXES

Alas, the woe and cost!

CHORUS

Alas, ye heavenly powers!
Ye wrought a sorrow past belief,
A woe, of woes the chief!
With aspect stern, upon us Ate looms!

XERXES

Smitten are we—time tells no heavier blow!

CHORUS

Smitten! the doom is plain!

XERXES

Curse upon curse and pang on pang we know!

CHORUS

With the Ionian power
We clashed, in evil hour!
Woe falls on Persia's race, yea, woe again, again!

XERXES

Yea, smitten am I, and my host is all to ruin hurled!

CHORUS

Yea verily—in mighty wreck hath sunk the Persian world!

XERXES (*holding up a torn robe and a quiver*)

See you this tattered rag of pride?

CHORUS

I see it, welladay!

XERXES

See you this quiver?

CHORUS

Say, hath aught survived and 'scaped the fray?

XERXES

A store for darts it was, erewhile!

CHORUS

Remain but two or three!

XERXES

No aid is left!

CHORUS

Ionian folk such darts, unfearing, see!

XERXES

Right resolute they are! I saw disaster unforeseen.

CHORUS

Ah, speakest thou of wreck, of flight, of carnage that hath been?

XERXES

Yea, and my royal robe I rent, in terror at their fall!

CHORUS

Alas, alas!

XERXES

Yea, thrice alas!

CHORUS

For all have perished, all!

XERXES

Ah woe to us, ah joy to them who stood against our pride!

CHORUS

And all our strength is minished and sundered from our side!

XERXES

No escort have I!

CHORUS

Nay, thy friends are whelmed beneath the tide!

XERXES

Wail, wail the miserable doom, and to the palace hie!

CHORUS

Alas, alas, and woe again!

XERXES

Shriek, smite the breast, as I!

CHORUS

An evil gift, a sad exchange, of tears poured out in vain!

XERXES

Shrill out your simultaneous wail!

CHORUS

Alas the woe and pain!

XERXES

O, bitter is this adverse fate!

CHORUS

I voice the moan with thee!

XERXES

Smite, smite thy bosom, groan aloud for my calamity!

CHORUS

I mourn and am dissolved in tears!

XERXES

Cry, beat thy breast amain!

CHORUS

O king, my heart is in thy woe!

XERXES

Shriek, wail, and shriek again!

CHORUS

O agony!

XERXES

A blackening blow—

CHORUS

A grievous stripe shall fall!

XERXES

Yea, beat anew thy breast, ring out the doleful Mysian call!

CHORUS

An agony, an agony!

XERXES

Pluck out thy whitening beard!

CHORUS

By handfuls, ay, by handfuls, with dismal tear-drops smeared!

XERXES

Sob out thine aching sorrow!

CHORUS

I will thine best obey.

XERXES

With thine hands rend thy mantle's fold—

CHORUS

Alas, woe worth the day!

XERXES

With thine own fingers tear thy locks, bewail the army's weird!

CHORUS

By handfuls, yea, by handfuls, with tears of dole besmeared!

XERXES

Now let thine eyes find overflow—

CHORUS

I wend in wail and pain!

XERXES

Cry out for me an answering moan—

CHORUS

Alas, alas again!

XERXES

Shriek with a cry of agony, and lead the doleful train!

CHORUS

Alas, alas, the Persian land is woeful now to tread!

XERXES

Cry out and mourn! the city now doth wail above the dead!

CHORUS

I sob and moan!

XERXES

I bid ye now be delicate in grief!

CHORUS

Alas, the Persian land is sad and knoweth not relief!

XERXES

Alas, the triple banks of oars and those who died thereby!

CHORUS

Pass! I will lead you, bring you home, with many a broken sigh!
[*Exeunt*

THE SEVEN AGAINST THEBES

DRAMATIS PERSONAE

ETEOCLES.
A SPY.
CHORUS OF CADMEAN MAIDENS.
ANTIGONE.
ISMENE.
A HERALD.

ETEOCLES

Clansmen of Cadmus, at the signal given
By time and season must the ruler speak
Who sets the course and steers the ship of State
With hand upon the tiller, and with eye
Watchful against the treachery of sleep.
For if all go aright, *thank Heaven*, men say,
But if adversely—which may God forefend!—
One name on many lips, from street to street,
Would bear the bruit and rumour of the time,
Down with Eteocles!—a clamorous curse,
A dirge of ruin. May averting Zeus
Make good his title here, in Cadmus' hold!
You it beseems now boys unripened yet
To lusty manhood, men gone past the prime
And increase of the full begetting seed,
And those whom youth and manhood well combined
Array for action—all to rise in aid
Of city, shrines, and altars of all powers
Who guard our land; that ne'er, to end of time,
Be blotted out the sacred service due
To our sweet mother-land and to her brood.
For she it was who to their guest-right called
Your waxing youth, was patient of the toil,
And cherished you on the land's gracious lap,
Alike to plant the hearth and bear the shield
In loyal service, for an hour like this.

91

Mark now! until to-day, luck rules our scale;
For we, though long beleaguered, in the main
Have with our sallies struck the foemen hard.
But now the seer, the feeder of the birds,
(Whose art unerring and prophetic skill
Of ear and mind divines their utterance
Without the lore of fire interpreted)
Foretelleth, by the mastery of his art,
That now an onset of Achaea's host
Is by a council of the night designed
To fall in double strength upon our walls.
Up and away, then, to the battlements,
The gates, the bulwarks! don your panoplies,
Array you at the breast-work, take your stand
On floorings of the towers, and with good heart
Stand firm for sudden sallies at the gates,
Nor hold too heinous a respect for hordes
Sent on you from afar: some god will guard!
I too, for shrewd espial of their camp,
Have sent forth scouts, and confidence is mine
They will not fail nor tremble at their task,
And, with their news, I fear no foeman's guile.
[*Enter* A SPY.

THE SPY

Eteocles, high king of Cadmus' folk,
I stand here with news certified and sure
From Argos' camp, things by myself descried.
Seven warriors yonder, doughty chiefs of might,
Into the crimsoned concave of a shield
Have shed a bull's blood, and, with hands immersed
Into the gore of sacrifice, have sworn
By Ares, lord of fight, and by thy name,
Blood-lapping Terror, *Let our oath be heard—*
Either to raze the walls, make void the hold
Of Cadmus—strive his children as they may—
Or, dying here, to make the foemen's land
With blood impasted. Then, as memory's gift
Unto their parents at the far-off home,
Chaplets they hung upon Adrastus' car,
With eyes tear-dropping, but no word of moan.
For their steeled spirit glowed with high resolve,

As lions pant, with battle in their eyes.
For them, no weak alarm delays the clear
Issues of death or life! I parted thence
Even as they cast the lots, how each should lead,
Against which gate, his serried company.
Rank then thy bravest, with what speed thou may'st,
Hard by the gates, to dash on them, for now,
Full-armed, the onward ranks of Argos come!
The dust whirls up, and from their panting steeds
White foamy flakes like snow bedew the plain.
Thou therefore, chieftain! like a steersman skilled,
Enshield the city's bulwarks, ere the blast
Of war comes darting on them! hark, the roar
Of the great landstorm with its waves of men!
Take Fortune by the forelock! for the rest,
By yonder dawn-light will I scan the field
Clear and aright, and surety of my word
Shall keep thee scatheless of the coming storm.

ETEOCLES

O Zeus and Earth and city-guarding gods,
And thou, my father's Curse, of baneful might,
Spare ye at least this town, nor root it up,
By violence of the foemen, stock and stem!
For here, from home and hearth, rings Hellas' tongue.
Forbid that e'er the yoke of slavery
Should bow this land of freedom, Cadmus' hold!
Be ye her help! your cause I plead with mine —
A city saved doth honour to her gods!
[*Exit* ETEOCLES, *etc. Enter the* CHORUS OF MAIDENS.

CHORUS

I wail in the stress of my terror,
and shrill is my cry of despair.
The foemen roll forth from their camp
as a billow, and onward they bear!
Their horsemen are swift in the forefront,
the dust rises up to the sky,
A signal, though speechless, of doom,
a herald more clear than a cry!
Hoof-trampled, the land of my love

bears onward the din to mine ears.
As a torrent descending a mountain,
it thunders and echoes and nears!
The doom is unloosened and cometh!
O kings and O queens of high Heaven,
Prevail that it fall not upon us:
the sign for their onset is given—
They stream to the walls from without,
white-shielded and keen for the fray.
They storm to the citadel gates—
what god or what goddess can stay
The rush of their feet? to what shrine
shall I bow me in terror and pray?
O gods high-throned in bliss,
we must crouch at the shrines in your home!
Not here must we tarry and wail:
shield clashes on shield as they come—
And now, even now is the hour
for the robes and the chaplets of prayer!
Mine eyes feel the flash of the sword,
the clang is instinct with the spear!
Is thy hand set against us, O Ares,
in ruin and wrath to o'erwhelm
Thine own immemorial land,
O god of the golden helm?
Look down upon us, we beseech thee,
on the land that thou lovest of old,
And ye, O protecting gods,
in pity your people behold!
Yea, save us, the maidenly troop,
from the doom and despair of the slave,
For the crests of the foemen come onward,
their rush is the rush of a wave
Rolled on by the war-god's breath!
almighty one, hear us and save
From the grasp of the Argives' might!
to the ramparts of Cadmus they crowd,
And, clenched in the teeth of the steeds,
the bits clink horror aloud!
And seven high chieftains of war,
with spear and with panoply bold,
Are set, by the law of the lot,
to storm the seven gates of our hold!

Be near and befriend us, O Pallas,
the Zeus-born maiden of might!
O lord of the steed and the sea,
be thy trident uplifted to smite
In eager desire of the fray, Poseidon!
and Ares come down,
In fatherly presence revealed,
to rescue Harmonia's town!
Thine too, Aphrodite, we are!
thou art mother and queen of our race,
To thee we cry out in our need,
from thee let thy children have grace!
Ye too, to scare back the foe,
be your cry as a wolf's howl wild,
Thou, O the wolf-lord, and thou,
of she-wolf Leto the child!
Woe and alack for the sound,
for the rattle of cars to the wall,
And the creak of the grinding axles!
O Hera, to thee is our call!
Artemis, maiden beloved!
the air is distraught with the spears,
And whither doth destiny drive us,
and where is the goal of our fears?
The blast of the terrible stones
on the ridge of our wall is not stayed,
At the gates is the brazen clash
of the bucklers—Apollo to aid!
Thou too, O daughter of Zeus,
who guidest the wavering fray
To the holy decision of fate,
Athena! be with us to-day!
Come down to the sevenfold gates
and harry the foemen away!
O gods and O sisters of gods,
our bulwark and guard! we beseech
That ye give not our war-worn hold
to a rabble of alien speech!
List to the call of the maidens,
the hands held up for the right,
Be near us, protect us, and show
that the city is dear in your sight!

Have heed for her sacrifice holy,
and thought of her offerings take,
Forget not her love and her worship,
be near her and smite for her sake!
[*Re-enter* ETEOCLES.
ETEOCLES

Hark to my question, things detestable!
Is this aright and for the city's weal,
And helpful to our army thus beset,
That ye before the statues of our gods
Should fling yourselves, and scream and shriek your fears?
Immodest, uncontrolled! Be this my lot—
Never in troublous nor in peaceful days
To dwell with aught that wears a female form!
Where womankind has power, no man can house,
Where womankind feeds panic, ruin rules
Alike in house and city! Look you now—
Your flying feet, and rumour of your fears,
Have spread a soulless panic on our walls,
And they without do go from strength to strength,
And we within make breach upon ourselves!
Such fate it brings, to house with womankind.
Therefore if any shall resist my rule—
Or man, or woman, or some sexless thing—
The vote of sentence shall decide their doom,
And stones of execution, past escape,
Shall finish all. Let not a woman's voice
Be loud in council! for the things without,
A man must care; let women keep within—
Even then is mischief all too probable!
Hear ye? or speak I to unheeding ears?

CHORUS

Ah, but I shudder, child of Oedipus!
I heard the clash and clang!
The axles rolled and rumbled; woe to us
Fire-welded bridles rang!

ETEOCLES

Say—when a ship is strained and deep in brine,
Did e'er a seaman mend his chance, who left
The helm, t'invoke the image at the prow?

CHORUS

Ah, but I fled to the shrines, I called to our helpers on high,
When the stone-shower roared at the portals!
I sped to the temples aloft, and loud was my call and my cry,
Look down and deliver. Immortals!

ETEOCLES

Ay, pray amain that stone may vanquish steel!
Were not that grace of gods? ay, ay—methinks,
When cities fall, the gods go forth from them!

CHORUS

Ah, let me die, or ever I behold
The gods go forth, in conflagration dire!
The foemen's rush and raid, and all our hold
Wrapt in the burning fire!

ETEOCLES

Cry not: on Heaven, in impotent debate!
What saith the saw?—*Good saving Strength, in verity,*
Out of Obedience breeds the babe Prosperity.

CHORUS

'Tis true: yet stronger is the power divine,
And oft, when man's estate is overbowed
With bitter pangs, disperses from his eyne
The heavy, hanging cloud!

ETEOCLES

Let men with sacrifice and augury
Approach the gods, when comes the tug of war;
Maids must be silent and abide within.

CHORUS

By grace of the gods we hold it,
a city untamed of the spear,
And the battlement wards from the wall
the foe and his aspect of fear!
What need of displeasure herein?

ETEOCLES

Ay, pay thy vows to Heaven; I grudge them not,
But—so thou strike no fear into our men—
Have calm at heart, nor be too much afraid.

CHORUS

Alack, it is fresh in mine ears,
the clamour and crash of the fray,
And up to our holiest height
I sped on my timorous way,
Bewildered, beset by the din!

ETEOCLES

Now, if ye hear the bruit of death or wounds,
Give not yourselves o'ermuch to shriek and scream,
For Ares ravens upon human flesh.

CHORUS

Ah, but the snorting of the steeds I hear!

ETEOCLES

Then, if thou hearts, hear them not too well!

CHORUS

Hark, the earth rumbles, as they close us round!

ETEOCLES

Enough if I am here, with plans prepared.

CHORUS

Alack, the battering at the gates is loud!

ETEOCLES

Peace! stay your tongue, or else the town may hear!

CHORUS

O warders of the walls, betray them not!

ETEOCLES

Bestrew your cries! in silence face your fate.

CHORUS

Gods of our city, see me not enslaved!

ETEOCLES

On me, on all, thy cries bring slavery.

CHORUS

Zeus, strong to smite, turn upon foes thy blow!

ETEOCLES

Zeus, what a curse are women, wrought by thee!

CHORUS

Weak wretches, even as men, when cities fall.

ETEOCLES

What! clasping gods, yet voicing thy despair?

CHORUS

In the sick heart, fear machete prey of speech.

ETEOCLES

Light is the thing I ask thee—do my will!

CHORUS

Ask swiftly: swiftly shall I know my power.

ETEOCLES

Silence, weak wretch! nor put thy friends in fear.

CHORUS

I speak no more: the general fate be mine!

ETEOCLES

I take that word as wiser than the rest.
Nay, more: these images possess thy will—
Pray, in their strength, that Heaven be on our side!
Then hear my prayers withal, and then ring out
The female triumph-note, thy privilege—
Yea, utter forth the usage Hellas knows,
The cry beside the altars, sounding clear
Encouragement to friends, alarm to foes.
But I unto all gods that guard our walls,
Lords of the plain or warders of the mart
And to Isthmus' stream and Dirge's rills,
I swear, if Fortune smiles and saves our town,
That we will make our altars reek with blood
Of sheep and kine, shed forth unto the gods,
And with victorious tokens front our fannies—
Corsets and cases that once our foemen wore,
Spear-shattered now—to deck these holy homes!

Be such thy vows to Heaven—away with sighs,
Away with outcry vain and barbarous,
That shall avail not, in a general doom!
But I will back, and, with six chosen men
Myself the seventh, to confront the foe
In this great aspect of a poised war,
Return and plant them at the sevenfold gates,
Or e'er the prompt and clamorous battle-scouts
Haste to inflame our counsel with the need.
[*Exit* ETEOCLES.

CHORUS

I mark his words, yet, dark and deep,
My heart's alarm forbiddeth sleep!
Close-clinging cares around my soul
Enkindle fears beyond control,
Presageful of what doom may fall
From the great leaguer of the wall!
So a poor dove is faint with fear
For her weak nestlings, while anew
Glides on the snaky ravisher!
In troop and squadron, hand on hand,
They climb and throng, and hemmed we stand,
While on the warders of our town
The flinty shower comes hurtling down!

Gods born of Zeus! put forth your might
For Cadmus' city, realm, and right!
What nobler land shall e'er be yours,
If once ye give to hostile powers
The deep rich soil, and Dirce's wave,
The nursing stream, Poseidon gave
And Tethys' children? Up and save!
Cast on the ranks that hem us round
A deadly panic, make them fling
Their arms in terror on the ground,
And die in carnage! thence shall spring
High honour for our clan and king!
Come at our wailing cry, and stand
As throned sentries of our land!

For pity and sorrow it were
that this immemorial town
Should sink to be slave of the spear,
to dust and to ashes gone down,
By the gods of Achaean worship
and arms of Achaean might
Sacked and defiled and dishonoured,
its women the prize of the fight —
That, haled by the hair as a steed,
their mantles dishevelled and torn,
The maiden and matron alike
should pass to the wedlock of scorn!
I hear it arise from the city,
the manifold wail of despair —
Woe, woe for the doom that shall be —
as in grasp of the foeman they fare!
For a woe and a weeping it is,
if the maiden inviolate flower
Is plucked by the foe in his might,
not culled in the bridal bower!
Alas for the hate and the horror —
how say it? — less hateful by far
Is the doom to be slain by the sword,
hewn down in the carnage of war!
For wide, ah! wide is the woe
when the foeman has mounted the wall;
There is havoc and terror and flame,
and the dark smoke broods over all,
And wild is the war-god's breath,
as in frenzy of conquest he springs,
And pollutes with the blast of his lips
the glory of holiest things!

Up to the citadel rise clash and din,
The war-net closes in,
The spear is in the heart: with blood imbrued
Young mothers wail aloud,
For children at their breast who scream and die!
And boys and maidens fly,
Yet scape not the pursuer, in his greed
To thrust and grasp and feed!
Robber with robber joins, each calls his mate
Unto the feast of hate —

The banquet, lo! is spread—
seize, rend, and tear!
No need to choose or share!
And all the wealth of earth to waste is poured—
A sight by all abhorred!
The grieving housewives eye it;
heaped and blent,
Earth's boons are spoiled and spent,
And waste to nothingness; and O alas,
Young maids, forlorn ye pass—
Fresh horror at your hearts—beneath the power
Of those who crop the flower!
Ye own the ruffian ravisher for lord,
And night brings rites abhorred!
Woe, woe for you! upon your grief and pain
There comes a fouler stain.
[*Enter, on one side,* THE SPY;
on the other, ETEOCLES
and the SIX CHAMPIONS.

SEMI-CHORUS

Look, friends! methinks the scout, who parted hence
To spy upon the foemen, comes with news,
His feet as swift as wafting chariot-wheels.

SEMI-CHORUS

Ay, and our king, the son of Oedipus,
Comes prompt to time, to learn the spy's report—
His heart is fainter than his foot is fast!

THE SPY

Well have I scanned the foe, and well can say
Unto which chief, by lot, each gate is given.
Tydeus already with his onset-cry
Storms at the gate called Proetides; but him
The seer Amphiaraus holds at halt,
Nor wills that he should cross Ismenus' ford,
Until the sacrifices promise fair.
But Tydeus, mad with lust of blood and broil,
Like to a cockatrice at noontide hour,

Hisses out wrath and smites with scourge of tongue
The prophet-son of Oecleus—*Wise thou art,*
Faint against war, and holding back from death!
With such revilings loud upon his lips
He waves the triple plumes that o'er his helm
Float overshadowing, as a courser's mane;
And at his shield's rim, terror in their tone,
Clang and reverberate the brazen bells.
And this proud sign, wrought on his shield, he bears—
The vault of heaven, inlaid with blazing stars;
And, for the boss, the bright moon glows at full,
The eye of night, the first and lordliest star.
Thus with high-vaunted armour, madly bold,
He clamours by the stream-bank, wild for war,
As a steed panting grimly on his bit,
Held in and chafing for the trumpet's bray!
Whom wilt thou set against him? when the gates
Of Proetus yield, who can his rush repel?

ETEOCLES

To me, no blazon on a foeman's shield
Shall e'er present a fear! such pointed threats
Are powerless to wound; his plumes and bells,
Without a spear, are snakes without a sting.
Nay, more—that pageant of which thou tellest—
The nightly sky displayed, ablaze with stars,
Upon his shield, palters with double sense—
One headstrong fool will find its truth anon!
For, if night fall upon his eyes in death,
Yon vaunting blazon will its own truth prove,
And he is prophet of his folly's fall.
Mine shall it be, to pit against his power
The loyal son of Astacus, as guard
To hold the gateways—a right valiant soul,
Who has in heed the throne of Modesty
And loathes the speech of Pride, and evermore
Shrinks from the base, but knows no other fear.
He springs by stock from those whom Ares spared,
The men called Sown, a right son of the soil,
And Melanippus styled. Now, what his arm
To-day shall do, rests with the dice of war,
And Ares shall ordain it; but his cause

Hath the true badge of Right, to urge him on
To guard, as son, his motherland from wrong.

CHORUS

Then may the gods give fortune fair
Unto our chief, sent forth to dare
War's terrible arbitrament!
But ah! when champions wend away,
I shudder, lest, from out the fray,
Only their blood-stained wrecks be sent!

THE SPY

Nay, let him pass, and the gods' help be his!
Next, Capaneus comes on, by lot to lead
The onset at the gates Electran styled:
A giant he, more huge than Tydeus' self,
And more than human in his arrogance—
May fate forefend his threat against our walls!
God willing, or unwilling—such his vaunt—
I will lay waste this city; Pallas' self,
Zeus' warrior maid, although she swoop to earth
And plant her in my path, shall stay me not.
And, for the flashes of the levin-bolt,
He holds them harmless as the noontide rays.
Mark, too, the symbol on his shield—a man
Scornfully weaponless but torch in hand,
And the flame glows within his grasp, prepared
For ravin: lo, the legend, wrought in words,
Fire for the city bring I, flares in gold!
Against such wight, send forth—yet whom? what man
Will front that vaunting figure and not fear?

ETEOCLES

Aha, this profits also, gain on gain!
In sooth, for mortals, the tongue's utterance
Bewrays unerringly a foolish pride!
Hither stalks Capaneus, with vaunt and threat
Defying god-like powers, equit to act,
And, mortal though he be, he strains his tongue
In folly's ecstasy, and casts aloft

105

High swelling words against the ears of Zeus.
Right well I trust—if justice grants the word—
That, by the might of Zeus, a bolt of flame
In more than semblance shall descend on him.
Against his vaunts, though reckless, I have set,
To make assurance sure, a warrior stern—
Strong Polyphontes, fervid for the fray;
A sturdy bulwark, he, by grace of Heaven
And favour of his champion Artemis!
Say on, who holdeth the next gate in ward?

CHORUS

Perish the wretch whose vaunt affronts our home!
On him the red bolt come,
Ere to the maiden bowers his way he cleave,
To ravage and bereave!

THE SPY

I will say on. Eteoclus is third—
To him it fell, what time the third lot sprang
O'er the inverted helmet's brazen rim,
To dash his stormers on Neistae gate.
He wheels his mares, who at their frontlets chafe
And yearn to charge upon the gates amain.
They snort the breath of pride, and, filled therewith,
Their nozzles whistle with barbaric sound.
High too and haughty is his shield's device—
An armed man who climbs, from rung to rung,
A scaling ladder, up a hostile wall,
Afire to sack and slay; and he too cries,
(By letters, full of sound, upon the shield)
Not Ares' self shall cast me from the wall.
Look to it, send, against this man, a man
Strong to debar the slave's yoke from our town.
ETEOCLES (*pointing to* MEGAREUS)

Send will I—even this man, with luck to aid—
By his worth sent already, not by pride
And vain pretence, is he. 'Tis Megareus,
The child of Creon, of the Earth-sprung born!
He will not shrink from guarding of the gates,

106

Nor fear the maddened charger's frenzied neigh,
But, if he dies, will nobly quit the score
For nurture to the land that gave him birth,
Or from the shield-side hew two warriors down
Eteoclus and the figure that he lifts—
Ay, and the city pictured, all in one,
And deck with spoils the temple of his sire!
Announce the next pair, stint not of thy tongue!

CHORUS

O thou, the warder of my home,
Grant, unto us, Fate's favouring tide,
Send on the foemen doom!
They fling forth taunts of frenzied pride,
On them may Zeus with glare of vengeance come;

THE SPY

Lo, next him stands a fourth and shouts amain,
By Pallas Onca's portal, and displays
A different challenge; 'tis Hippomedon!
Huge the device that starts up from his targe
In high relief; and, I deny it not,
I shuddered, seeing how, upon the rim,
It made a mighty circle round the shield—
No sorry craftsman he, who wrought that work
And clamped it all around the buckler's edge!
The form was Typhon: from his glowing throat
Rolled lurid smoke, spark-litten, kin of fire!
The flattened edge-work, circling round the whole,
Made strong support for coiling snakes that grew
Erect above the concave of the shield:
Loud rang the warrior's voice; inspired for war,
He raves to slay, as doth a Bacchanal,
His very glance a terror! of such wight
Beware the onset! closing on the gates,
He peals his vaunting and appalling cry!

ETEOCLES

Yet first our Pallas Onca—wardress she,
Planting her foot hard by her gate—shall stand,
The Maid against the ruffian, and repel
His force, as from her brood the mother-bird
Beats back the wintered serpent's venom'd fang
And next, by her, is Oenops' gallant son,
Hyperbius, chosen to confront this foe,
Ready to seek his fate at Fortune's shrine!

In form, in valour, and in skill of arms,
None shall gainsay him. See how wisely well
Hermes hath set the brave against the strong!
Confronted shall they stand, the shield of each
Bearing the image of opposing gods:
One holds aloft his Typhon breathing fire,
But, on the other's shield, in symbol sits
Zeus, calm and strong, and fans his bolt to flame—
Zeus, seen of all, yet seen of none to fail!
Howbeit, weak is trust reposed in Heaven—
Yet are we upon Zeus' victorious side,
The foe, with those he worsted—if in sooth
Zeus against Typhon held the upper hand,
And if Hyperbius, (as well may hap
When two such foes such diverse emblems bear)
Have Zeus upon his shield, a saving sign.

CHORUS

High faith is mine that he whose shield
Bears, against Zeus, the thing of hate.
The giant Typhon, thus revealed,
A monster loathed of gods eterne
And mortal men—this doom shall earn
A shattered skull, before the gate!

THE SPY

Heaven send it so!
A fifth assailant now
Is set against our fifth, the northern, gate,
Fronting the death-mound where Amphion lies
The child of Zeus.

This foeman vows his faith,
Upon a mystic spear-head which he deems
More holy than a godhead and more sure
To find its mark than any glance of eye,
That, will they, nill they, he will storm and sack
The hold of the Cadmeans. Such his oath—
His, the bold warrior, yet of childish years,
A bud of beauty's foremost flower, the son
Of Zeus and of the mountain maid. I mark
How the soft down is waxing on his cheek,
Thick and close-growing in its tender prime—
In name, not mood, is he a maiden's child—
Parthenopaeus; large and bright his eyes
But fierce the wrath wherewith he fronts the gate:
Yet not unheralded he takes his stand
Before the portal; on his brazen shield,
The rounded screen and shelter of his form,
I saw him show the ravening Sphinx, the fiend
That shamed our city—how it glared and moved,
Clamped on the buckler, wrought in high relief!
And in its claws did a Cadmean bear—
Nor heretofore, for any single prey,
Sped she aloft, through such a storm of darts
As now awaits her. So our foe is here—
Like, as I deem, to ply no stinted trade
In blood and broil, but traffick as is meet
In fierce exchange for his long wayfaring!

ETEOCLES

Ah, may they meet the doom they think to bring—
They and their impious vaunts—from those on high!
So should they sink, hurled down to deepest death!
This foe, at least, by thee Arcadian styled,
Is faced by one who bears no braggart sign,
But his hand sees to smite, where blows avail—
Actor, own brother to Hyperbius!
He will not let a boast without a blow
Stream through our gates and nourish our despair,
Nor give him way who on his hostile shield
Bears the brute image of the loathly Sphinx!
Blocked at the gate, she will rebuke the man
Who strives to thrust her forward, when she feels
Thick crash of blows, up to the city wall.
With Heaven's goodwill, my forecast shall be true.

CHORUS

Home to my heart the vaunting goes,
And, quick with terror, on my head
Rises my hair, at sound of those
Who wildly, impiously rave!
If gods there be, to them I plead—
Give them to darkness and the grave.

THE SPY

Fronting the sixth gate stands another foe,
Wisest of warriors, bravest among seers—
Such must I name Amphiaraus: he,
Set steadfast at the Homoloid gate,
Berates strong Tydeus with reviling words—
The man of blood, the bane of state and home,
To Argos, arch-allurer to all ill,
Evoker of the fury-fiend of hell,
Death's minister, and counsellor of wrong
Unto Adrastus in this fatal field.
Ay, and with eyes upturned and mien of scorn
He chides thy brother Polynices too
At his desert, and once and yet again
Dwells hard and meaningly upon his name

Where it saith *glory* yet importeth *feud*.
Yea, such thou art in act, and such thy grace
In sight of Heaven, and such in aftertime
Thy fame, for lips and ears of mortal men!
"He strove to sack the city of his sires
And temples of her gods, and brought on her
An alien armament of foreign foes.
The fountain of maternal blood outpoured
What power can staunch? even so, thy fatherland
Once by thine ardent malice stormed and ta'en,
Shall ne'er join force with thee." For me, I know
It doth remain to let my blood enrich
The border of this land that loves me not —
Blood of a prophet, in a foreign grave!
Now, for the battle! I foreknow my doom,
Yet it shall be with honour. So he spake,
The prophet, holding up his targe of bronze
Wrought without blazon, to the ears of men
Who stood around and heeded not his word.
For on no bruit and rumour of great deeds,
But on their doing, is his spirit set,
And in his heart he reaps a furrow rich,
Wherefrom the foison of good counsel springs.
Against him, send brave heart and hand of might,
For the god-lover is man's fiercest foe.

ETEOCLES

Out on the chance that couples mortal men,
Linking the just and impious in one!
In every issue, the one curse is this—
Companionship with men of evil heart!
A baneful harvest, let none gather it!
The field of sin is rank, and brings forth death
At whiles a righteous man who goes aboard
With reckless mates, a horde of villainy,
Dies by one death with that detested crew;
At whiles the just man, joined with citizens
Ruthless to strangers, recking nought of Heaven,
Trapped, against nature, in one net with them,
Dies by God's thrust and all-including blow.
So will this prophet die, even Oecleus' child,
Sage, just, and brave, and loyal towards Heaven,

Potent in prophecy, but mated here
With men of sin, too boastful to be wise!
Long is their road, and they return no more,
And, at their taking-off, by hand of Zeus,
The prophet too shall take the downward way.
He will not—so I deem—assail the gate—
Not as through cowardice or feeble will,
But as one knowing to what end shall be
Their struggle in the battle, if indeed
Fruit of fulfilment lie in Loxias' word.
He speaketh not, unless to speak avails!
Yet, for more surety, we will post a man,
Strong Lasthenes, as warder of the gate,
Stern to the foeman; he hath age's skill,
Mated with youthful vigour, and an eye
Forward, alert; swift too his hand, to catch
The fenceless interval 'twixt shield and spear!
Yet man's good fortune lies in hand of Heaven.

CHORUS

Unto our loyal cry, ye gods, give ear!
Save, save the city! turn away the spear,
Send on the foemen fear!
Outside the rampart fall they, rent and riven
Beneath the bolt of heaven!

THE SPY

Last, let me name yon seventh antagonist,
Thy brother's self, at the seventh portal set—
Hear with what wrath he imprecates our doom,
Vowing to mount the wall, though banished hence,
And peal aloud the wild exulting cry—
The town is ta'en—then clash his sword with thine,
Giving and taking death in close embrace,
Or, if thou 'scapest, flinging upon thee,
As robber of his honour and his home,
The doom of exile such as he has borne.
So clamours he and so invokes the gods
Who guard his race and home, to hear and heed
The curse that sounds in Polynices' name!
He bears a round shield, fresh from forge and fire,

And wrought upon it is a twofold sign—
For lo, a woman leads decorously
The figure of a warrior wrought in gold;
And thus the legend runs—*I Justice am,*
And I will bring the hero home again,
To hold once more his place within this town,
Once more to pace his sire's ancestral hall.
Such are the symbols, by our foemen shown—
Now make thine own decision, whom to send
Against this last opponent! I have said—
Nor canst thou in my tidings find a flaw—
Thine is it, now, to steer the course aright.

ETEOCLES

Ah me, the madman, and the curse of Heaven!
And woe for us, the lamentable line
Of Oedipus, and woe that in this house
Our father's curse must find accomplishment!
But now, a truce to tears and loud lament,
Lest they should breed a still more rueful wail!
As for this Polynices, named too well,
Soon shall we know how his device shall end—
Whether the gold-wrought symbols on his shield,
In their mad vaunting and bewildered pride,
Shall guide him as a victor to his home!
For had but Justice, maiden-child of Zeus,
Stood by his act and thought, it might have been!
Yet never, from the day he reached the light
Out of the darkness of his mother's womb,
Never in childhood, nor in youthful prime,
Nor when his chin was gathering its beard,
Hath Justice hailed or claimed him as her own.
Therefore I deem not that she standeth now
To aid him in this outrage on his home!
Misnamed, in truth, were Justice, utterly,
If to impiety she lent her hand.
Sure in this faith, I will myself go forth
And match me with him; who hath fairer claim?
Ruler, against one fain to snatch the rule,
Brother with brother matched, and foe with foe,
Will I confront the issue. To the wall!

CHORUS

O thou true heart, O child of Oedipus,
Be not, in wrath, too like the man whose name
Murmurs an evil omen! 'Tis enough
That Cadmus' clan should strive with Argos' host,
For blood there is that can atone that stain!
But—brother upon brother dealing death—
Not time itself can expiate the sin!

ETEOCLES

If man find hurt, yet clasp his honour still,
'Tis well; the dead have honour, nought beside.
Hurt, with dishonour, wins no word of praise!

CHORUS

Ah, what is thy desire?
Let not the lust and ravin of the sword
Bear thee adown the tide accursed, abhorred!
Fling off thy passion's rage, thy spirit's prompting dire!

ETEOCLES

Nay—since the god is urgent for our doom,
Let Laius' house, by Phoebus loathed and scorned,
Follow the gale of destiny, and win
Its great inheritance, the gulf of hell!

CHORUS

Ruthless thy craving is—
Craving for kindred and forbidden blood
To be outpoured—a sacrifice imbrued
With sin, a bitter fruit of murderous enmities!

ETEOCLES

Yea, my own father's fateful Curse proclaims—
A ghastly presence, and her eyes are dry—
Strike! honour is the prize, not life prolonged!

114

CHORUS

Ah, be not urged of her! for none shall dare
To call thee *coward*, in thy throned estate!
Will not the Fury in her sable pall
Pass outward from these halls, what time the gods
Welcome a votive offering from our hands?

ETEOCLES

The gods! long since they hold us in contempt,
Scornful of gifts thus offered by the lost!
Why should we fawn and flinch away from doom?

CHORUS

Now, when it stands beside thee! for its power
May, with a changing gust of milder mood,
Temper the blast that bloweth wild and rude
And frenzied, in this hour!

ETEOCLES

Ay, kindled by the curse of Oedipus—
All too prophetic, out of dreamland came
The vision, meting out our sire's estate!

CHORUS

Heed women's voices, though thou love them not!

ETEOCLES

Say aught that may avail, but stint thy words.

CHORUS

Go not thou forth to guard the seventh gate!

ETEOCLES

Words shall not blunt the edge of my resolve.

CHORUS

Yet the god loves to let the weak prevail.

ETEOCLES

That to a swordsman, is no welcome word!

CHORUS

Shall thine own brother's blood be victory's palm?

ETEOCLES

Ill which the gods have sent thou canst not shun!
[*Exit* ETEOCLES. CHORUS

I shudder in dread of the power,
abhorred by the gods of high heaven,
The ruinous curse of the home
till roof-tree and rafter be riven!
Too true are the visions of ill,
too true the fulfilment they bring
To the curse that was spoken of old
by the frenzy and wrath of the king!
Her will is the doom of the children,
and Discord is kindled amain,
And strange is the Lord of Division,
who cleaveth the birthright in twain,—
The edged thing, born of the north,
the steel that is ruthless and keen,
Dividing in bitter division
the lot of the children of teen!
Not the wide lowland around,
the realm of their sire, shall they have,
Yet enough for the dead to inherit,
the pitiful space of a grave!

Ah, but when kin meets kin, when sire and child,
Unknowing, are defiled
By shedding common blood, and when the pit
Of death devoureth it,
Drinking the clotted stain, the gory dye—

Who, who can purify?
Who cleanse pollution, where the ancient bane
Rises and reeks again?
Whilome in olden days the sin was wrought,
And swift requital brought—
Yea on the children of the child came still
New heritage of ill!
For thrice Apollo spoke this word divine,
From Delphi's central shrine,
To Laius—*Die thou childless*! thus alone
Can the land's weal be won!
But vainly with his wife's desire he strove,
And gave himself to love,
Begetting Oedipus, by whom he died,
The fateful parricide!
The sacred seed-plot, his own mother's womb,
He sowed, his house's doom,
A root of blood! by frenzy lured, they came
Unto their wedded shame.
And now the waxing surge, the wave of fate,
Rolls on them, triply great—
One billow sinks, the next towers, high and dark,
Above our city's bark—
Only the narrow barrier of the wall
Totters, as soon to fall;
And, if our chieftains in the storm go down,
What chance can save the town?
Curses, inherited from long ago,
Bring heavy freight of woe:
Rich stores of merchandise o'erload the deck,
Near, nearer comes the wreck—
And all is lost, cast out upon the wave,
Floating, with none to save!

Whom did the gods, whom did the chief of men,
Whom did each citizen
In crowded concourse, in such honour hold,
As Oedipus of old,
When the grim fiend, that fed on human prey,
He took from us away?

But when, in the fulness of days,
he knew of his bridal unblest,

117

A twofold horror he wrought,
in the frenzied despair of his breast—
Debarred from the grace of the banquet,
the service of goblets of gold,
He flung on his children a curse
for the splendour they dared to withhold,
A curse prophetic and bitter—
The glory of wealth and of pride,
With iron, not gold, in your hands,
ye shall come, at the last, to divide!
Behold, how a shudder runs through me,
lest now, in the fulness of time,
The house-fiend awake and return,
to mete out the measure of crime!
[*Enter* THE SPY.

THE SPY

Take heart, ye daughters whom your mothers' milk
Made milky-hearted! lo, our city stands,
Saved from the yoke of servitude: the vaunts
Of overweening men are silent now,
And the State sails beneath a sky serene,
Nor in the manifold and battering waves
Hath shipped a single surge, and solid stands
The rampart, and the gates are made secure,
Each with a single champion's trusty guard.
So in the main and at six gates we hold
A victory assured; but, at the seventh,
The god that on the seventh day was born,
Royal Apollo, hath ta'en up his rest
To wreak upon the sons of Oedipus
Their grandsire's wilfulness of long ago.

CHORUS

What further woefulness besets our home?

THE SPY

The home stands safe—but ah, the princes twain—

118

CHORUS

Who? what of them? I am distraught with fear.

THE SPY

Hear now, and mark! the sons of Oedipus—

CHORUS

Ah, my prophetic soul! I feel their doom.

THE SPY

Have done with questions!—with their lives crushed out—

CHORUS

Lie they out yonder? the full horror speak!
Did hands meet hands more close than brotherly?
Came fate on each, and in the selfsame hour?

THE SPY

Yea, blotting out the lineage ill-starred!
Now mix your exultation and your tears,
Over a city saved, the while its lords,
Twin leaders of the fight, have parcelled out
With forged arbitrament of Scythian steel
The full division of their fatherland,
And, as their father's imprecation bade,
Shall have their due of land, a twofold grave.
So is the city saved; the earth has drunk
Blood of twin princes, by each other slain.

CHORUS

O mighty Zeus and guardian powers,
The strength and stay of Cadmus' towers!
Shall I send forth a joyous cry,
Hail to the lord of weal renewed?
Or weep the misbegotten twain,
Born to a fatal destiny?
Each numbered now among the slain,
Each dying in ill fortitude,
Each *truly named*, each *child of feud?*

O dark and all-prevailing ill,
That broods o'er Oedipus and all his line,
Numbing my heart with mortal chill!
Ah me, this song of mine,
Which, Thyad-like, I woke, now falleth still,
Or only tells of doom,
And echoes round a tomb!

Dead are they, dead! in their own blood they lie—
Ill-omened the concent that hails our victory!
The curse a father on his children spake
Hath faltered not, nor failed!
Nought, Laius! thy stubborn choice availed—
First to beget, then, in the after day
And for the city's sake,
The child to slay!
For nought can blunt nor mar
The speech oracular!
Children of teen! by disbelief ye erred—
Yet in wild weeping came fulfilment of the word!
[ANTIGONE *and* ISMENE *approach,*
with a train of mourners, bearing the
bodies of ETEOCLES *and* POLYNICES.

Look up, look forth! the doom is plain,
Nor spake the messenger in vain!
A twofold sorrow, twofold strife—
Each brave against a brother's life!
In double doom hath sorrow come—
How shall I speak it?—on the home!

120

The Suppliant Maidens and Other Plays

Alas, my sisters! be your sighs the gale,
The smiting of your brows the plash of oars,
Wafting the boat, to Acheron's dim shores
That passeth ever, with its darkened sail,
On its uncharted voyage and sunless way,
Far from thy beams, Apollo, god of day—
The melancholy bark
Bound for the common bourn, the harbour of the dark!
Look up, look yonder! from the home
Antigone, Ismene come,
On the last, saddest errand bound,
To chant a dirge of doleful sound,
With agony of equal pain
Above their brethren slain!
Their sister-bosoms surely swell,
Heart with rent heart according well
In grief for those who fought and fell!
Yet—ere they utter forth their woe—
We must awake the rueful strain
To vengeful powers, in realms below,
And mourn hell's triumph o'er the slain!

Alas! of all, the breast who bind,—
Yea, all the race of womankind—
O maidens, ye are most bereaved!
For you, for you the tear-drops start—
Deem that in truth, and undeceived,
Ye hear the sorrows of my heart!
(*To the dead.*)
Children of bitterness, and sternly brave—
One, proud of heart against persuasion's voice,
One, against exile proof! ye win your choice—
Each in your fatherland, a separate grave!

Alack, on house and heritage
They brought a baneful doom, and death for wage!
One strove through tottering walls to force his way,
One claimed, in bitter arrogance, the sway,
And both alike, even now and here,
Have closed their suit, with steel for arbiter!
And lo, the Fury-fiend of Oedipus, their sire,
Hath brought his curse to consummation dire!
Each in the left side smitten, see them laid—

The children of one womb,
Slain by a mutual doom!
Alas, their fate! the combat murderous,
The horror of the house,
The curse of ancient bloodshed, now repaid!
Yea, deep and to the heart the deathblow fell,
Edged by their feud ineffable —
By the grim curse, their sire did imprecate —
Discord and deadly hate!
Hark, how the city and its towers make moan —
How the land mourns that held them for its own!
Fierce greed and fell division did they blend,
Till death made end!
They strove to part the heritage in twain,
Giving to each a gain —
Yet that which struck the balance in the strife,
The arbitrating sword,
By those who loved the twain is held abhorred —
Loathed is the god of death, who sundered each from life!
Here, by the stroke of steel, behold! they lie —
And rightly may we cry
Beside their fathers, let them here be laid —
Iron gave their doom, with iron their graves be made —
Alack, the slaying sword, alack, th' entombing spade!

Alas, a piercing shriek, a rending groan,
A cry unfeigned of sorrow felt at heart!
With shuddering of grief, with tears that start,
With wailful escort, let them hither come —
For one or other make divided moan!
No light lament of pity mixed with gladness,
But with true tears, poured from the soul of sadness,
Over the princes dead and their bereaved home

Say we, above these brethren dead,
On citizen, on foreign foe,
Brave was their rush, and stern their blow —
Now, lowly are they laid!
Beyond all women upon earth
Woe, woe for her who gave them birth!
Unknowingly, her son she wed —
The children of that marriage-bed,
Each in the self-same womb, were bred —

Each by a brother's hand lies dead!

Yea, from one seed they sprang, and by one fate
Their heritage is desolate,
The heart's division sundered claim from claim,
And, from their feud, death came!
Now is their hate allayed,
Now is their life-stream shed,
Ensanguining the earth with crimson dye—
Lo, from one blood they sprang, and in one blood they lie!
A grievous arbiter was given the twain—
The stranger from the northern main,
The sharp, dividing sword,
Fresh from the forge and fire
The War-god treacherous gave ill award
And brought their father's curse to a fulfilment dire!
They have their portion—each his lot and doom,
Given from the gods on high!
Yea, the piled wealth of fatherland, for tomb,
Shall underneath them lie!
Alas, alas! with flowers of fame and pride
Your home ye glorified;
But, in the end, the Furies gathered round
With chants of boding sound,

Shrieking, *In wild defeat and disarray,*
Behold, ye pass away!
The sign of Ruin standeth at the gate,
There, where they strove with Fate—
And the ill power beheld the brothers' fall,
And triumphed over all!
ANTIGONE, ISMENE, *and* CHORUS
(*Processional Chant*)

Thou wert smitten, in smiting,
Thou didst slay, and wert slain—
By the spear of each other
Ye lie on the plain,
And ruthless the deed that ye wrought was,
and ruthless the death of the twain!

Take voice, O my sorrow!
Flow tear upon tear—

Lay the slain by the slayer,
Made one on the bier!
Our soul in distraction is lost,
and we mourn o'er the prey of the spear!

Ah, woe for your ending,
Unbrotherly wrought!
And woe for the issue,
The fray that ye fought,
The doom of a mutual slaughter
whereby to the grave ye are brought!

Ah, twofold the sorrow—
The heard and the seen!
And double the tide
Of our tears and our teen,
As we stand by our brothers in death
and wail for the love that has been!

O grievous the fate
That attends upon wrong!
Stern ghost of our sire,
Thy vengeance is long!
Dark Fury of hell and of death, the hands of thy
kingdom are strong!

O dark were the sorrows
That exile hath known!
He slew, but returned not
Alive to his own!
He struck down a brother, but fell, in the moment of
triumph hewn down!

O lineage accurst,
O doom and despair!
Alas, for their quarrel,
The brothers that were!
And woe! for their pitiful end, who once were our
love and our care!

O grievous the fate
That attends upon wrong!
Stern ghost of our sire,

Thy vengeance is long!
Dark Fury of hell and of death, the hands of thy
kingdom are strong!

By proof have ye learnt it!
At once and as one,
O brothers beloved,
To death ye were done!
Ye came to the strife of the sword, and behold! ye
are both overthrown!

O grievous the tale is,
And grievous their fall,
To the house, to the land,
And to me above all!
Ah God! for the curse that hath come, the sin and
the ruin withal!

O children distraught,
Who in madness have died!
Shall ye rest with old kings
In the place of their pride?
Alas for the wrath of your sire if he findeth you laid
by his side!
[*Enter a* HERALD.

HERALD

I bear command to tell to one and all
What hath approved itself and now is law,
Ruled by the counsellors of Cadmus' town.
For this Eteocles, it is resolved
To lay him on his earth-bed, in this soil,
Not without care and kindly sepulture.
For why? he hated those who hated us,
And, with all duties blamelessly performed
Unto the sacred ritual of his sires,
He met such end as gains our city's grace,—
With auspices that do ennoble death.
Such words I have in charge to speak of him:
But of his brother Polynices, this—
Be he cast out unburied, for the dogs
To rend and tear: for he presumed to waste

The land of the Cadmeans, had not Heaven—
Some god of those who aid our fatherland—
Opposed his onset, by his brother's spear,
To whom, tho' dead, shall consecration come!
Against him stood this wretch, and brought a horde
Of foreign foemen, to beset our town.
He therefore shall receive his recompense,
Buried ignobly in the maw of kites—
No women-wailers to escort his corpse
Nor pile his tomb nor shrill his dirge anew—
Unhouselled, unattended, cast away!
So, for these brothers, doth our State ordain.

ANTIGONE

And I—to those who make such claims of rule
In Cadmus' town—I, though no other help,
(*Pointing to the body of* POLYNICES)
I, I will bury this my brother's corse
And risk your wrath and what may come of it!
It shames me not to face the State, and set
Will against power, rebellion resolute:
Deep in my heart is set my sisterhood,
My common birthright with my brothers, born
All of one womb, her children who, for woe,
Brought forth sad offspring to a sire ill-starred.
Therefore, my soul! take thou thy willing share,
In aid of him who now can will no more,
Against this outrage: be a sister true,
While yet thou livest, to a brother dead!
Him never shall the wolves with ravening maw
Rend and devour: I do forbid the thought!
I for him, I—albeit a woman weak—
In place of burial-pit, will give him rest
By this protecting handful of light dust
Which, in the lap of this poor linen robe,
I bear to hallow and bestrew his corpse
With the due covering. Let none gainsay!
Courage and craft shall arm me, this to do.

HERALD

I charge thee, not to flout the city's law!

126

ANTIGONE

I charge thee, use no useless heralding!

HERALD

Stern is a people newly 'scaped from death.

ANTIGONE

Whet thou their sternness! Burial he shall have.

HERALD

How? Grace of burial, to the city's foe?

ANTIGONE

God hath not judged him separate in guilt.

HERALD

True—till he put this land in jeopardy.

ANTIGONE

His rights usurped, he answered wrong with wrong.

HERALD

Nay—but for one man's sin he smote the State.

ANTIGONE

Contention doth out-talk all other gods!
Prate thou no more—I will to bury him.

HERALD

Will, an thou wilt! but I forbid the deed.
[*Exit* the HERALD.

CHORUS

Exulting Fates, who waste the line
And whelm the house of Oedipus!
Fiends, who have slain, in wrath condign,
The father and the children thus!
What now befits it that I do,
What meditate, what undergo?
Can I the funeral rite refrain,
Nor weep for Polynices slain?
But yet, with fear I shrink and thrill,
Presageful of the city's will!
Thou, O Eteocles, shalt have
Full rites, and mourners at thy grave,
But he, thy brother slain, shall he,
With none to weep or cry *Alas*,
To unbefriended burial pass?
Only one sister o'er his bier,
To raise the cry and pour the tear—
Who can obey such stern decree?

SEMI-CHORUS

Let those who hold our city's sway
Wreak, or forbear to wreak, their will
On those who cry, *Ah, well-a-day!*
Lamenting Polynices still!
We will go forth and, side by side
With her, due burial will provide!
Royal he was; to him be paid
Our grief, wherever he be laid!
The crowd may sway, and change, and still
Take its caprice for Justice' will!
But we this dead Eteocles,
As Justice wills and Right decrees,
Will bear unto his grave!
For—under those enthroned on high
And Zeus' eternal royalty—
He unto us salvation gave!
He saved us from a foreign yoke,—
A wild assault of outland folk,
A savage, alien wave!
[*Exeunt.*

PROMETHEUS BOUND

ARGUMENT

In the beginning, Ouranos and Gaia held sway over Heaven and Earth. And manifold children were born unto them, of whom were Cronos, and Okeanos, and the Titans, and the Giants. But Cronos cast down his father Ouranos, and ruled in his stead, until Zeus his son cast him down in his turn, and became King of Gods and men. Then were the Titans divided, for some had good will unto Cronos, and others unto Zeus; until Prometheus, son of the Titan Iapetos, by wise counsel, gave the victory to Zeus. But Zeus held the race of mortal men in scorn, and was fain to destroy them from the face of the earth; yet Prometheus loved them, and gave secretly to them the gift of fire, and arts whereby they could prosper upon the earth. Then was Zeus sorely angered with Prometheus, and bound him upon a mountain, and afterward overwhelmed him in an earthquake, and devised other torments against him for many ages; yet could he not slay Prometheus, for he was a God.

DRAMATIS PERSONAE

STRENGTH AND FORCE.
HEPHAESTUS.
PROMETHEUS.
CHORUS OF SEA-NYMPHS,
DAUGHTERS OF OCEANUS.
OCEANUS.
IO.
HERMES.

Scene—A rocky ravine in the mountains of Scythia.

STRENGTH

Lo, the earth's bound and limitary land,
The Scythian steppe, the waste untrod of men!
Look to it now, Hephaestus—thine it is,
Thy Sire obeying, this arch-thief to clench
Against the steep-down precipice of rock,
With stubborn links of adamantine chain.
Look thou: thy flower, the gleaming plastic fire,
He stole and lent to mortal man—a sin
That gods immortal make him rue to-day,
Lessoned hereby to own th' omnipotence
Of Zeus, and to repent his love to man!

HEPHAESTUS

O Strength and Force, for you the best of Zeus
Stands all achieved, and nothing bars your will:
But I—I dare not bind to storm-vext cleft
One of our race, immortal as are we.
Yet, none the less, necessity constrains,
For Zeus, defied, is heavy in revenge!
(*To PROMETHEUS*)

O deep-devising child of Themis sage,
Small will have I to do, or thou to bear,
What yet we must. Beyond the haunt of man
Unto this rock, with fetters grimly forged,

I must transfix and shackle up thy limbs,
Where thou shalt mark no voice nor human form,
But, parching in the glow and glare of sun,
Thy body's flower shall suffer a sky-change;
And gladly wilt thou hail the hour when Night
Shall in her starry robe invest the day,
Or when the Sun shall melt the morning rime.
But, day or night, for ever shall the load
Of wasting agony, that may not pass,
Wear thee away; for know, the womb of Time
Hath not conceived a power to set thee free.
Such meed thou hast, for love toward mankind
For thou, a god defying wrath of gods,
Beyond the ordinance didst champion men,
And for reward shalt keep a sleepless watch,
Stiff-kneed, erect, nailed to this dismal rock,
With manifold laments and useless cries
Against the will inexorable of Zeus.
Hard is the heart of fresh-usurped power!

STRENGTH

Enough of useless ruth! why tarriest thou?
Why pitiest one whom all gods wholly hate,
One who to man gave o'er thy privilege?

HEPHAESTUS

Kinship and friendship wring my heart for him.

STRENGTH

Ay—but how disregard our Sire's command?
Is not thy pity weaker than thy fear?

HEPHAESTUS

Ruthless as ever, brutal to the full!

STRENGTH

Tears can avail him nothing: strive not thou,
Nor waste thine efforts thus unaidingly.

HEPHAESTUS

Out on my cursed mastery of steel!

STRENGTH

Why curse it thus? In sooth that craft of thine
Standeth assoiled of all that here is wrought.

HEPHAESTUS

Would that some other were endowed therewith!

STRENGTH

All hath its burden, save the rule of Heaven,
And freedom is for Zeus, and Zeus alone.

HEPHAESTUS

I know it; I gainsay no word hereof.

STRENGTH

Up, then, and hasten to do on his bonds,
Lest Zeus behold thee indolent of will!

HEPHAESTUS

Ah well—behold the armlets ready now!

STRENGTH

Then cast them round his arms and with sheer strength
Swing down the hammer, clinch him to the crags.

HEPHAESTUS

Lo, 'tis toward—no weakness in the work!

STRENGTH

Smite harder, wedge it home—no faltering here!
He hath a craft can pass th' impassable!

HEPHAESTUS

This arm is fast, inextricably bound.

STRENGTH

Then shackle safe the other, that he know
His utmost craft is weaker far than Zeus.

HEPHAESTUS

He, but none other, can accuse mine art!

STRENGTH

Now, strong and sheer, drive thro' from breast to back
The adamantine wedge's stubborn fang.

HEPHAESTUS

Alas, Prometheus! I lament thy pain.

STRENGTH

Thou, faltering and weeping sore for those
Whom Zeus abhors! 'ware, lest thou rue thy tears!

HEPHAESTUS

Thou gazest on a scene that poisons sight.

STRENGTH

I gaze on one who suffers his desert.
Now between rib and shoulder shackle him—

HEPHAESTUS

Do it I must—hush thy superfluous charge!

STRENGTH

Urge thee I will—ay, hound thee to the prey.
Step downward now, enring his legs amain!

HEPHAESTUS

Lo, it is done—'twas but a moment's toil.

STRENGTH

Now, strongly strike, drive in the piercing gyves—
Stern is the power that oversees thy task!

HEPHAESTUS

Brutish thy form, thy speech brutality!

STRENGTH

Be gentle, an thou wilt, but blame not me
For this my stubbornness and anger fell!

HEPHAESTUS

Let us go hence; his legs are firmly chained.

STRENGTH (*To* PROMETHEUS)

Aha! there play the insolent, and steal,
For creatures of a day, the rights of gods!
O deep delusion of the powers that named thee
Prometheus, the Fore-thinker! thou hast need
Of others' forethought and device, whereby
Thou may'st elude this handicraft of ours!
[*Exeunt* HEPHAESTUS, STRENGTH,
and FORCE. —*A pause.*

PROMETHEUS

O Sky divine, O Winds of pinions swift,
O fountain-heads of Rivers, and O thou,
Illimitable laughter of the Sea!
O Earth, the Mighty Mother, and thou Sun,
Whose orbed light surveyeth all—attest,
What ills I suffer from the gods, a god!
Behold me, who must here sustain
The marring agonies of pain,
Wrestling with torture, doomed to bear
Eternal ages, year on year!
Such and so shameful is the chain
Which Heaven's new tyrant doth ordain
To bind me helpless here.
Woe! for the ruthless present doom!
Woe! for the Future's teeming womb!
On what far dawn, in what dim skies,
Shall star of my deliverance rise?

Truce to this utterance! to its dimmest verge
I do foreknow the future, hour by hour,
Nor can whatever pang may smite me now
Smite with surprise. The destiny ordained
I must endure to the best, for well I wot
That none may challenge with Necessity.
Yet is it past my patience, to reveal,
Or to conceal, these issues of my doom.
Since I to mortals brought prerogatives,
Unto this durance dismal am I bound:
Yea, I am he who in a fennel-stalk,
By stealthy sleight, purveyed the fount of fire,
The teacher, proven thus, and arch-resource
Of every art that aideth mortal men.
Such was my sin: I earn its recompense,
Rock-riveted, and chained in height and cold.
[*A pause.*
Listen! what breath of sound,
what fragrance soft hath risen
Upward to me? is it some godlike essence,
Or being half-divine, or mortal presence?
Who to the world's end comes, unto my craggy prison?
Craves he the sight of pain, or what would he behold?

135

Gaze on a god in tortures manifold,
Heinous to Zeus, and scorned by all
Whose footsteps tread the heavenly hall,
Because too deeply, from on high,
I pitied man's mortality!
Hark, and again! that fluttering sound
Of wings that whirr and circle round,
And their light rustle thrills the air—
How all things that unseen draw near
Are to me Fear!
[*Enter the* CHORUS OF OCEANIDES,
in winged cars]
CHORUS

Ah, fear us not! as friends, with rivalry
Of swiftly-vying wings, we came together
Unto this rock and thee!
With our sea-sire we pleaded hard, until
We won him to our will,
And swift the wafting breezes bore us hither.
The heavy hammer's steely blow
Thrilled to our ocean-cavern from afar,
Banished soft shyness from our maiden brow,
And with unsandalled feet we come, in winged car!

PROMETHEUS

Ah well-a-day! ye come, ye come
From the Sea-Mother's teeming home—
Children of Tethys and the sire
Who around Earth rolls, gyre on gyre,
His sleepless ocean-tide!
Look on me—shackled with what chain,
Upon this chasm's beetling side
I must my dismal watch sustain!

CHORUS

Yea, I behold, Prometheus! and my fears
Draw swiftly o'er mine eyes a mist fulfilled of tears,
When I behold thy frame
Bound, wasting on the rock, and put to shame
By adamantine chains!
The rudder and the rule of Heaven
Are to strange pilots given:
Zeus with new laws and strong caprice holds sway,
Unkings the ancient Powers, their might constrains,
And thrusts their pride away!

PROMETHEUS

Had he but hurled me, far beneath
The vast and ghostly halls of Death,
Down to the limitless profound Of Tartarus,
in fetters bound, Fixed by his unrelenting hand!
So had no man, nor God on high,
Exulted o'er mine agony—
But now, a sport to wind and sky,
Mocked by my foes, I stand!

CHORUS

What God can wear such ruthless heart
As to delight in ill?
Who in thy sorrow bears not part?
Zeus, Zeus alone! for he, with wrathful will,
Clenched and inflexible,
Bears down Heaven's race—nor end shall be, till hate
His soul shall satiate,
Or till, by some device, some other hand
Shall wrest from him his sternly-clasped command!

PROMETHEUS

Yet,—though in shackles close and strong
I lie in wasting torments long, —-
Yet the new tyrant, 'neath whose nod
Cowers down each blest subservient god,
One day, far hence, my help shall need,

The destined stratagem to read,
Whereby, in some yet distant day,
Zeus shall be reaved of pride and sway:
And no persuasion's honied spell
Shall lure me on, the tale to tell;
And no stern threat shall make me cower
And yield the secret to his power,
Until his purpose be foregone,
And shackles yield, and he atone
The deep despite that he hath done!

CHORUS

O strong in hardihood, thou striv'st amain
Against the stress of pain!
But yet too free, too resolute thy tongue
In challenging thy wrong!
Ah, shuddering dread doth make my spirit quiver,
And o'er thy fate sits Fear!
I see not to what shore of safety ever
Thy bark can steer—
In depths unreached the will of Zeus doth dwell,
Hidden, implacable!

PROMETHEUS

Ay, stern is Zeus, and Justice stands,
Wrenched to his purpose, in his hands—
Yet shall he learn, perforce, to know
A milder mood, when falls the blow—
His ruthless wrath he shall lay still,
And he and I with mutual will
In concord's bond shall go.

CHORUS

Unveil, say forth to us the tale entire,
Under what imputation Zeus laid hands
On thee, to rack thee thus with shameful pangs?
Tell us—unless the telling pain thee—all!

PROMETHEUS

Grievous alike are these things for my tongue,
Grievous for silence—rueful everyway.
Know that, when first the gods began their strife,
And heaven was all astir with mutual feud—
Some willing to fling Cronos from his throne,
And set, forsooth, their Zeus on high as king,
And other some in contrariety
Striving to bar him from heaven's throne for aye—
Thereon I sought to counsel for the best
The Titan brood of Ouranos and Earth;
Yet I prevailed not, for they held in scorn
My glozing wiles, and, in their hardy pride,
Deemed that sans effort they could grasp the sway.
But, for my sake, my mother Themis oft,
And Earth, one symbol of names manifold,
Had held me warned, how in futurity
It stood ordained that not by force or power,
But by some wile, the victors must prevail.
In such wise I interpreted; but they
Deigned not to cast their heed thereon at all.
Then, of things possible, I deemed it best,
Joining my mother's wisdom to mine own,
To range myself with Zeus, two wills in one.
Thus, by device of mine, the murky depth
Of Tartarus enfoldeth Cronos old
And those who strove beside him. Such the aid
I gave the lord of heaven—my meed for which
He paid me thus, a penal recompense!
For 'tis the inward vice of tyranny,
To deem of friends as being secret foes.
Now, to your question—hear me clearly show
On what imputed fault he tortures me.
Scarce was he seated on his father's throne,
When he began his doles of privilege
Among the lesser gods, allotting power
In trim division; while of mortal men
Nothing he recked, nor of their misery
Nay, even willed to blast their race entire
To nothingness, and breed another brood;
And none but I was found to cross his will.
I dared it, I alone; I rescued men

From crushing ruin and th' abyss of hell—
Therefore am I constrained in chastisement
Grievous to bear and piteous to behold,—
Yea, firm to feel compassion for mankind,
Myself was held unworthy of the same—
Ay, beyond pity am I ranged and ruled
To sufferance—a sight that shames his sway!

CHORUS

A heart of steel, a mould of stone were he,
Who could complacently behold thy pains
I came not here as craving for this sight,
And, seeing it, I stand heart-wrung with pain.

PROMETHEUS

Yea truly, kindly eyes must pity me!

CHORUS

Say, didst thou push transgression further still?

PROMETHEUS

Ay, man thro' me ceased to foreknow his death.

CHORUS

What cure couldst thou discover for this curse?

PROMETHEUS

Blind hopes I sent to nestle in man's heart.

CHORUS

This was a goodly gift thou gavest them.—

PROMETHEUS

Yet more I gave them, even the boon of fire.

CHORUS

What? radiant fire, to things ephemeral?

PROMETHEUS

Yea—many an art too shall they learn thereby!

CHORUS

Then, upon imputation of such guilt,
Doth Zeus without surcease torment thee thus?
Is there no limit to thy course of pain?

PROMETHEUS

None, till his own will shall decree an end.

CHORUS

And how shall he decree it? say, what hope?
Seest thou not thy sin? yet of that sin
It irks me sore to speak, as thee to hear.
Nay, no more words hereof; bethink thee now,
From this ordeal how to find release.

PROMETHEUS

Easy it is, for one whose foot is set
Outside the slough of pain, to lesson well
With admonitions him who lies therein.
With perfect knowledge did I all I did,
I willed to sin, and sinned, I own it all—
I championed men, unto my proper pain.
Yet scarce I deemed that, in such cruel doom,
Withering upon this skyey precipice,
I should inherit lonely mountain crags,
Here, in a vast tin-neighboured solitude.
Yet list not to lament my present pains,
But, stepping from your cars unto the ground,
Listen, the while I tell the future fates
Now drawing near, until ye know the whole.
Grant ye, O grant my prayer, be pitiful

To one now racked with woe! the doom of pain
Wanders, but settles, soon or late, on all.

CHORUS

To willing hearts, and schooled to feel,
Prometheus, came thy tongue's appeal;
Therefore we leave, with lightsome tread,
The flying cars in which we sped—
We leave the stainless virgin air
Where winged creatures float and fare,
And by thy side, on rocky land,
Thus gently we alight and stand,
Willing, from end to end, to know
Thine history of woe.
[*The* CHORUS *alight from their winged cars.*
Enter OCEANUS, *mounted on a griffin.*
OCEANUS

Thus, over leagues and leagues of space
I come, Prometheus, to thy place—
By will alone, not rein, I guide
The winged thing on which I ride;
And much, be sure, I mourn thy case—
Kinship is Pity's bond, I trow;
And, wert thou not akin, I vow
None other should have more than thou
Of my compassion's grace!
'Tis said, and shall be proved; no skill
Have I to gloze and feign goodwill!
Name but some mode of helpfulness,
And thou wilt in a trice confess
That I, Oceanus, am best
Of all thy friends, and trustiest.

PROMETHEUS

Ho, what a sight of marvel! what, thou too
Comest to contemplate my pains, and darest—
(Yet how, I wot not!) leaving far behind
The circling tide, thy namefellow, and those
Rock-arched, self-hollowed caverns—thus to come
Unto this land, whose womb bears iron ore?
Art come to see my lot, resent with me
The ills I bear? Well, gaze thy fill! behold
Me, friend of Zeus, part-author of his power—
Mark, in what ruthlessness he bows me down!

OCEANUS

Yea, I behold, Prometheus! and would warn
Thee, spite of all thy wisdom, for thy weal!
Learn now thyself to know, and to renew
A rightful spirit within thee, for, made new
With pride of place, sits Zeus among the gods!
Now, if thou choosest to fling forth on him
Words rough with anger thus and edged with scorn,
Zeus, though he sit aloof, afar, on high,
May hear thine utterance, and make thee deem
His present wrath a mere pretence of pain.
Banish, poor wretch! the passion of thy soul,
And seek, instead, acquittance from thy pangs!
Belike my words seem ancientry to thee—
Such, natheless, O Prometheus, is the meed
That doth await the overweening tongue!
Meek wert thou never, wilt not crouch to pain,
But, set amid misfortunes, cravest more!
Now—if thou let thyself be schooled by me—
Thou must not kick against the goad. Thou knowest,
A despot rules, harsh, resolute, supreme,
Whose law is will. Yet shall I go to him,
With all endeavour to relieve thy plight—
So thou wilt curb the tempest of thy tongue!
Surely thou knowest, in thy wisdom deep,
The saw—*Who vaunts amiss, quick pain is his.*

PROMETHEUS

O enviable thou, and unaccused—
Thou who wast art and part in all I dared!
And now, let be! make this no care of thine,
For Zeus is past persuasion—urge him not!
Look to thyself, lest thine emprise thou rue.

OCEANUS

Thou hast more skill to school thy neighbour's fault
Than to amend thine own: 'tis proved and plain,
By fact, not hearsay, that I read this well.
Yet am I fixed to go—withhold me not—
Assured I am, assured, that Zeus will grant
The boon I crave, the loosening of thy bonds.

PROMETHEUS

In part I praise thee, to the end will praise;
Goodwill thou lackest not, but yet forbear
Thy further trouble! If thy heart be fain,
Bethink thee that thy toil avails me not.
Nay, rest thee well, aloof from danger's brink!
I will not ease my woe by base relief
In knowing others too involved therein.
Away the thought! for deeply do I rue
My brother Atlas' doom. Far off he stands
In sunset land, and on his shoulder bears
The pillar'd mountain-mass whose base is earth,
Whose top is heaven, and its ponderous load
Too great for any grasp. With pity too
I saw Earth's child, the monstrous thing of war,
That in Cilicia's hollow places dwelt—
Typho; I saw his hundred-headed form
Crushed and constrained; yet once his stride was fierce,
His jaws gaped horror and their hiss was death,
And all heaven's host he challenged to the fray,
While, as one vowed to storm the power of Zeus,
Forth from his eyes he shot a demon glare.
It skilled not: the unsleeping bolt of Zeus,
The downward levin with its rush of flame,
Smote on him, and made dumb for evermore

The clamour of his vaunting: to the heart
Stricken he lay, and all that mould of strength
Sank thunder-shattered to a smouldering ash;
And helpless now and laid in ruin huge
He lieth by the narrow strait of sea,
Crushed at the root of Etna's mountain-pile.
High on the pinnacles whereof there sits
Hephaestus, sweltering at the forge; and thence
On some hereafter day shall burst and stream
The lava-floods, that shall with ravening fangs
Gnaw thy smooth lowlands, fertile Sicily!
Such ire shall Typho from his living grave
Send seething up, such jets of fiery surge,
Hot and unslaked, altho' himself be laid
In quaking ashes by Zeus' thunderbolt.
But thou dost know hereof, nor needest me
To school thy sense: thou knowest safety's road —
Walk then thereon! I to the dregs will drain,
Till Zeus relent from wrath, my present woe.

OCEANUS

Nay, but, Prometheus, know'st thou not the saw —
Words can appease the angry soul's disease?

PROMETHEUS

Ay — if in season one apply their salve,
Not scorching wrath's proud flesh with caustic tongue.

OCEANUS

But in wise thought and venturous essay
Perceivest thou a danger? prithee tell!

PROMETHEUS

I see a fool's good nature, useless toil.

OCEANUS

Let me be sick of that disease; I know,
Loyalty, masked as folly, wins the way.

PROMETHEUS

But of thy blunder I shall bear the blame.

OCEANUS

Clearly, thy word would send me home again.

PROMETHEUS

Lest thy lament for me should bring thee hate.

OCEANUS

Hate from the newly-throned Omnipotence?

PROMETHEUS

Be heedful—lest his will be wroth with thee!

OCEANUS

Thy doom, Prometheus, cries to me *Beware*!

PROMETHEUS

Mount, make away, discretion at thy side!

OCEANUS

Thy word is said to me in act to go:
For lo, my hippogriff with waving wings
Fans the smooth course of air, and fain is he
To rest his limbs within his ocean stall.
[*Exit* OCEANUS. CHORUS

For the woe and the wreck and the doom,
Prometheus I utter my sighs;
O'er my cheek flows the fountain of tears
from tender, compassionate eyes.
For stern and abhorred is the sway
of Zeus on his self-sought throne,
And ruthless the spear of his scorn,

146

to the gods of the days that are done.
And over the limitless earth
goes up a disconsolate cry:
Ye were all so fair, and have fallen;
so great and your might has gone by!
So wails with a mighty lament
the voice of the mortals, who dwell
In the Eastland, the home of the holy,
for thee and the fate that befel;
And they of the Colchian land, the
maidens whose arm is for war;
And the Scythian bowmen, who roam
by the lake of Maeotis afar;
And the blossom of battling hordes,
that flowers upon Caucasus' height,
With clashing of lances that pierce,
and with clamour of swords that smite.
Strange is thy sorrow! one only I know
who has suffered thy pain —
Atlas the Titan, the god,
in a ruthless, invincible chain!
He beareth for ever and ever
the burden and poise of the sky,
The vault of the rolling heaven,
and earth re-echoes his cry.
The depths of the sea are troubled;
they mourn from their caverns profound,
And the darkest and innermost hell
moans deep with a sorrowful sound;
And the rivers of waters, that flow
from the fountains that spring without stain,
Are as one in the great lamentation,
and moan for thy piteous pain.

PROMETHEUS

Deem not that I in pride or wilful scorn
Restrain my speech; 'tis wistful memory
That rends my heart, when I behold myself
Abased to wretchedness. To these new gods
I and none other gave their lots of power
In full attainment; no more words hereof
I speak — the tale ye know. But listen now

Unto the rede of mortals and their woes,
And how their childish and unreasoning state
Was changed by me to consciousness and thought.
Yet not in blame of mortals will I speak,
But as in proof of service wrought to them.
For, in the outset, eyes they had and saw not;
And ears they had but heard not; age on age,
Like unsubstantial shapes in vision seen,
They groped at random in the world of sense,
Nor knew to link their building, brick with brick,
Nor how to turn its aspect to the sun,
Nor how to join the beams by carpentry,
In hollowed caves they dwelt, as emmets dwell,
Weak feathers for each blast, in sunless caves.
Nor had they certain forecast of the cold,
Nor of the advent of the flowery spring,
Nor of the fruitful summer. All they wrought,
Unreasoning they wrought, till I made clear
The laws of rising stars, and inference dim,
More hard to learn, of what their setting showed.
I taught to them withal that art of arts,
The lore of number, and the written word
That giveth sense to sound, the tool wherewith
The gift of memory was wrought in all,
And so came art and song. I too was first
To harness 'neath the yoke strong animals,
Obedient made to collar and to weight,
That they might bear whate'er of heaviest toil
Mortals endured before. For chariots too
I trained, and docile service of the rein,
Steeds, the delight of wealth and pomp and pride.
I too, none other, for seafarers wrought
Their ocean-roaming canvas-winged cars.
Such arts of craft did I, unhappy I,
Contrive for mortals: now, no feint I have
Whereby I may elude my present woe.

CHORUS

A rueful doom is thine! distraught of soul,
And all astray, and like some sorry leech
Art thou, repining at thine own disease,
Unskilled, unknowing of the needful cure.

PROMETHEUS

More wilt thou wonder when the rest thou hearest—
What arts for them, what methods I devised.
Foremost was this: if any man fell sick,
No aiding art he knew, no saving food,
No curing oil nor draught, but all in lack
Of remedies they dwindled, till I taught
The medicinal blending of soft drugs,
Whereby they ward each sickness from their side.
I ranged for them the methods manifold
Of the diviner's art; I first discerned
Which of night's visions hold a truth for day,
I read for them the lore of mystic sounds,
Inscrutable before; the omens seen
Which bless or ban a journey, and the flight
Of crook-clawed birds, did I make clear to man—
And how they soar upon the right, for weal,
How, on the left, for evil; how they dwell,
Each in its kind, and what their loves and hates,
And which can flock and roost in harmony.
From me, men learned what deep significance
Lay in the smoothness of the entrails set
For sacrifice, and which, of various hues,
Showed them a gift accepted of the gods;
They learned what streaked and varied comeliness
Of gall and liver told; I led them, too,
(By passing thro' the flame the thigh-bones, wrapt
In rolls of fat, and th' undivided chine),
Unto the mystic and perplexing lore
Of omens; and I cleared unto their eyes
The forecasts, dim and indistinct before,
Shown in the flickering aspect of a flame.
Of these, enough is said. The other boons,
Stored in the womb of earth, in aid of men—
Copper and iron, silver, gold withal—
Who dares affirm he found them ere I found?
None—well I know—save who would babble lies!
Know thou, in compass of a single phrase—
All arts, for mortals' use, Prometheus gave.

CHORUS

Nay, aid not mortal men beyond their due,
Holding too light a reckoning of thyself
And of thine own distress: good hope have I
To see thee once again from fetters free
And matched with Zeus in parity of power.

PROMETHEUS

Not yet nor thus hath Fate ordained the end—
Not until age-long pains and countless woes
Have bent and bowed me, shall my shackles fall;
Art strives too feebly against destiny.

CHORUS

But what hand rules the helm of destiny?

PROMETHEUS

The triform Fates, and Furies unforgiving.

CHORUS

Then is the power of Zeus more weak than theirs?

PROMETHEUS

He may not shun the fate ordained for him.

CHORUS

What is ordained for him, save endless rule?

PROMETHEUS

Seek not for answer: this thou may'st not learn.

CHORUS

Surely thy silence hides some solemn thing.

PROMETHEUS

Think on some other theme: 'tis not the hour,
This secret to unveil; in deepest dark
Be it concealed: by guarding it shall I
Escape at last from bonds, and scorn, and pain.

CHORUS

O never may my weak and faint desire
Strive against God most high—
Never be slack in service, never tire
Of sacred loyalty;
Nor fail to wend unto the altar-side,
Where with the blood of kine
Steams up the offering, by the quenchless tide
Of Ocean, Sire divine!
Be this within my heart, indelible—
Offend not with thy tongue!
Sweet, sweet it is, in cheering hopes to dwell,
Immortal, ever young,
In maiden gladness fostering evermore
A soft content of soul!
But ah, I shudder at thine anguish sore—
Thy doom thro' years that roll!
Thou could'st not cower to Zeus: a love too great
Thou unto man hast given—
Too high of heart thou wert—ah, thankless fate!
What aid, 'gainst wrath of Heaven,
Could mortal man afford? in vain thy gift
To things so powerless!
Could'st thou not see? they are as dreams that drift;
Their strength is feebleness
A purblind race, in hopeless fetters bound,
They have no craft or skill,
That could o'erreach the ordinance profound
of the eternal will.
Alas, Prometheus! on thy woe condign
I looked, and learned this lore;
And a new strain floats to these lips of mine—
Not the glad song of yore,
When by the lustral wave I sang to see
My sister made thy bride,

151

Decked with thy gifts, thy loved Hesione,
And clasped unto thy side.
[*Enter* IO, *horned like a cow.*]

IO

Alack! what land, what folk are here?
Whom see I clenched in rocky fetters drear
Unto the stormy crag?
for what thing done
Dost thou in agony atone?
Ah, tell me whither, well-a-day!
My feet have roamed their weary way?
Ah, but it maddens, the sting!
it burns in my piteous side!
Ah, but the vision, the spectre,
the earth-born, the myriad-eyed!
Avoid thee! Earth, hide him,
thine offspring! he cometh—O aspect of ill!
Ghostly, and crafty of face,
and dead, but pursuing me still!
Ah, woe upon me, woe ineffable!
He steals upon my track, a hound of hell—
Where'er I stray, along the sands and brine,
Weary and foodless, come his creeping eyne!
And ah, the ghostly sound—
The wax-stopped reed-flute's weird and drowsy drone!
Alack my wandering woes, that round and round
Lead me in many mazes, lost, foredone!
O child of Cronos! for what deed of wrong
Am I enthralled by thee in penance long?
Why by the stinging bruise, the thing of fear,
Dost thou torment me, heart and brain?
Nay, give me rather to the flames that sear,
Or to some hidden grave,
Or to the rending jaws, the monsters of the main!
Nor grudge the boon for which I crave, O king!
Enough, enough of weary wandering,
Pangs from which none can save!
Hearken! in pity hold
Io, the ox-horned maid, thy love of old!

PROMETHEUS

Hear Zeus or not, I hear and know thee well,
Daughter of Inachus; I know thee driven,
Stung by the gadfly, mazed with agony.
Ay, thou art she whose beauty fired the breast
Of Zeus with passion; she whom Hera's hate
Now harasses o'er leagues and leagues of land.

IO

Alack, thou namest Inachus my sire!
Wottest thou of him? how, from lips of pain,
Comes to my woeful ears truth's very strain?
How knowest thou the curse, the burning fire
The god-sent, piercing pest that stings and clings?
Ah me! in frenzied, foodless wanderings
Hither I come, and on me from on high
Lies Hera's angry craft! Ah, men unblest!
Not one there is, not one, that is unblest as I.
But thou—tell me the rest!
Utter the rede of woes to come for me;
Utter the aid, the cure, if aid or cure there be!

PROMETHEUS

Lo, clearly will I show forth all thy quest—
Not in dark speech, but with such simple phrase
As doth befit the utterance of a friend.
I am Prometheus, who gave fire to men.

IO

O daring, proven champion of man's race,
What sin, Prometheus, dost thou thus atone?

PROMETHEUS

One moment since, I told my woes and ceased.

IO

Then should I plead my suit to thee in vain?

PROMETHEUS

Nay, speak thy need; nought would I hide from thee.

IO

Pronounce who nailed thee to the rocky cleft.

PROMETHEUS

Zeus, by intent; Hephaestus, by his hand.

IO

For what wrongdoing do these pains atone?

PROMETHEUS

What I have said, is said; suffice it thee!

IO

Yet somewhat add; forewarn me in my woe
What time shall bring my wandering to its goal?

PROMETHEUS

Fore-knowledge is fore-sorrow; ask it not.

IO

Nay, hide not from me destiny's decree.

PROMETHEUS

I grudge thee not the gift which I withhold.

IO

Then wherefore tarry ere thou tell me all?

PROMETHEUS

Nothing I grudge, but would not rack thy soul.

IO

Be not compassionate beyond my wish.

PROMETHEUS

Well, thou art fain, and I will speak. Attend!

CHORUS

Nay—ere thou speak, hear me, bestow on me
A portion of the grace of granted prayers.
First let us learn how Io's frenzy came—
(She telling her disasters manifold)
Then of their sequel let her know from thee.

PROMETHEUS

Well were it, Io, thus to do their will—
Right well! they are the sisters of thy sire.
'Tis worth the waste and effluence of time,
To tell, with tears of perfect moan, the doom
Of sorrows that have fallen, when 'tis sure
The listeners will greet the tale with tears.

IO

I know not how I should mistrust your prayer;
Therefore the whole that ye desire of me
Ye now shall learn in one straightforward tale.
Yet, as it leaves my lips, I blush with shame
To tell that tempest of the spite of Heaven,
And all the wreck and ruin of my form,
And whence they swooped upon me, woe is me!
Long, long in visions of the night there came
Voices and forms into my maiden bower,
Alluring me with smoothly glozing words—
O maiden highly favoured of high Heaven,
Why cherish thy virginity so long?

Thine is it to win wedlock's noblest crown!
Know that Zeus' heart thro' thee is all aflame,
Pierced with desire as with a dart, and longs
To join in utmost rite of love with thee.
Therefore, O maiden, shun not with disdain
Th' embrace of Zeus, but hie thee forth straightway
To the lush growth of Lerna's meadow-land,
Where are the flocks and steadings of thy home,
And let Zeus' eye be eased of its desire.
Night after night, haunted by dreams like these,
Heartsick, I ventured at the last to tell
Unto my sire these visions of the dark.
Then sent he many a wight, on sacred quest,
To Delphi and to far Dodona's shrine,
Being fall fain to learn what deed or word
Would win him favour from the powers of heaven.
But they came back repeating oracles
Mystic, ambiguous, inscrutable,
Till, at the last, an utterance direct,
Obscure no more, was brought to Inachus—
A peremptory charge to fling me forth
Beyond my home and fatherland, a thing
Sent loose in banishment o'er all the world;
And—should he falter—Zeus should launch on him
A fire-eyed bolt, to shatter and consume
Himself and all his race to nothingness.
Bowing before such utterance from the shrine
Of Loxias, he drave me from our halls,
Barring the gates against me: loth he was
To do, as I to suffer, this despite:
But the strong curb of Zeus had overborne
His will to me-ward. As I parted thence,
In form and mind I grew dishumanized,
And horned as now ye see me, poison-stung
By the envenomed bitings of the brize,
I leapt and flung in frenzy, rushed away
To the bright waters of Cerchneia's stream
And Lerna's beach: but ever at my side,
A herdsman by his heifer, Argus moved,
Earth-born, malevolent of mood, and peered,
With myriad eyes, where'er my feet would roam.
But on him in a moment, unforeseen,
Came Fate, and sundered him from life; but I,

Still maddened by the gadfly's sting, the scourge
Of God's infliction, roam the weary world.
How I have fared, thou hearest: be there aught
Of what remains to bear, that thou canst tell,
Speak on! but let not thy compassion warm
Thy words to cheering falsehood. Worst of woes
Are words that break their promise to our hope!

CHORUS

Woe! woe! avaunt—thou and thy tale of bane!
O never, never dared I dream
Such horror of strange sounds should pierce mine ear;
Such loathly sights, such tortures hard to bear,
Outrage, pollution, agony supreme,
Wasting my heart with double edge of pain!
Ah Fate, ah Fate! I gaze on Io's dole,
And shudder to my soul!

PROMETHEUS

Thou wailest all too soon, fulfilled of fear—
Tarry awhile, till thou have learned the whole.

CHORUS

Say on, reveal it! suffering souls are fain
To know aright what yet remains to bear.

PROMETHEUS

Lightly, with help of mine, did ye achieve
That which ye first desired: from Io's mouth
craved to hear, recounted by herself,
The story of her strivings. Listen now
To what shall follow, to what woefulness
The wrath of Hera must compel this maid.
(*To* Io)
And thou, O child of Inachus, within
Thine inmost heart store up these words of mine,
That thou may'st learn thy wanderings and their goal.
First from this spot toward the sunrise turn,
And cross the steppe that knoweth not the plough:

157

Thus to the nomad Scythians shalt thou come,
Who dwell in wattled homes, not built on earth
But borne along on wains of sturdy wheel—
Equipped, themselves, with bows of mighty reach.
Pass them avoidingly, and leave their land,
And skirt the beaches where the tides make moan,
Till lo! upon the left hand thou shalt find
The Chalybes, stout craftsmen of the steel—
Beware of them! no gentleness is theirs,
No kindly welcome to a stranger's foot!
Thence to the Stream of Violence shalt thou come—
Like name, like nature; see thou cross it not,
('Tis fatal to the forder!) till thou come
Right to the very Caucasus, the peak
That overtops the world, and from its brows
The river pants in spray its wrathful stream.
Thence, o'er the pinnacles that court the stars,
Onward and southward thou must take thy way,
And reach the warlike horde of Amazons,
Maidens through hate of man; and gladly they
Will guide thy maiden feet. That host, in days
That are not yet, shall fix their home and dwell
At Themiscyra, on Thermodon's bank,
Nigh whereunto the grim projecting fang
Of Salmydessus' cape affronts the main,
The seaman's curse, to ships a stepmother!
Then at the jutting land, Cimmerian styled,
That screens the narrowing portal of the mere,
Thou shalt arrive; pass o'er it, brave at heart,
And ferry thee across Macotis' ford.
So shall there be great rumour evermore,
In ears of mortals, of thy passage strange;
And Bosporos shall be that channel's name,
Because the ox-horned thing did pass thereby.
So, from the wilds of Europe wander'd o'er,
To Asia's continent thou com'st at last.
(*To the* CHORUS)
And ye, what think ye? Seems he not, that lord
And tyrant of the gods, as tyrannous
Unto all other lives? A high god's lust
Constrained this mortal maid to roam the world!
(*To* Io)
Poor maid! a brutal wooer sure was thine!

158

For know that all which I have told thee now
Is scarce the prelude of thy woes to come.

IO

Alas for me, alas!

PROMETHEUS

Again thou criest, with a heifer's low.
What wilt thou do, learning thy future woes?

CHORUS

What, hast thou further sorrows for her ear?

PROMETHEUS

Yea, a vext ocean of predestined pain.

IO

What profit then is life to me? Ah, why
Did I not cast me from this stubborn crag?
So with one spring, one crash upon the ground,
I had attained surcease from all my woes.
Better it is to die one death outright
Than linger out long life in misery.

PROMETHEUS

Ill would'st thou bear these agonies of mine—
Mine, with whose fate it standeth not to win
The goal of death, which were release from pain!
Now, there is set no limit to my woe
Till Zeus be hurled from his omnipotence.

IO

Zeus hurled from pride of place! Can such things be?

PROMETHEUS

Thou wert full fain, methinks, to see that sight!

IO

Even so—his overthrow who wrought my pain.

PROMETHEUS

Then may'st thou know thereof; such fall shall be.

IO

And who shall wrench the sceptre from his hand?

PROMETHEUS

By his own mindless counsels shall he fall.

IO

And how? unless the telling harm, say on!

PROMETHEUS

Wooing a bride, his ruin he shall win.

IO

Goddess, or mortal? tell me, if thou may'st.

PROMETHEUS

No matter which—more must not be revealed.

IO

Doth then a consort thrust him from his throne?

PROMETHEUS

The child she bears him shall o'ercome his sire.

IO

And hath he no avoidance of this doom?

PROMETHEUS

None, surely—till that I, released from bonds—

IO

Who can release thee, but by will of Zeus?

PROMETHEUS

Fate gives this duty to a child of thine!

IO

How? Shall a child of mine undo thy woes?

PROMETHEUS

Yea, of thy lineage, thirteen times removed.

IO

Dark beyond guessing grows thine oracle.

PROMETHEUS

Yea—seek not therefore to foreknow thy woes.

IO

As thou didst proffer hope, withdraw it not.

PROMETHEUS

Two tales I have—choose! for I grant thee one.

IO

And which be they? reveal, and leave me choice.

PROMETHEUS

I grant it: shall I in all clearness show
Thy future woes, or my deliverance?

CHORUS

Nay! of the two, vouchsafe her wish to her
And mine to me, deigning a truth to each—
To her, reveal her future wanderings—
To me, thy future saviour, as I crave!

PROMETHEUS

I will not set myself to thwart your will
Withholding aught of what ye crave to know.
First to thee, Io, will I tell and trace
Thy scared circuitous wandering mark it well,
Deep in retentive tablets of the soul.
When thou hast overpast the ferry's flow
That sunders continent from continent,
Straight to the eastward and the flaming face
Of dawn, and highways trodden by the sun,
Pass, till thou come unto the windy land
Of daughters born to Boreas: beware
Lest the strong spirit of the stormy blast
Snatch thee aloft, and sweep thee to the void,
On wings of raving wintry hurricane!
Wend by the noisy tumult of the wave,
Until thou reach the Gorgon-haunted plains
Beside Cisthene. In that solitude
Dwell Phorcys' daughters, beldames worn with time,
Three, each swan-shapen, single-toothed, and all
Peering thro' shared endowment of one eye;
Never on them doth the sun shed his rays,
Never falls radiance of the midnight moon.
But, hard by these, their sisters, clad with wings,
Serpentine-curled, dwell, loathed of mortal men,—
The Gorgons!—he of men who looks on them
Shall gasp away his life. Of such fell guard
I bid thee to beware. Now, mark my words
When I another sight of terror tell—
Beware the Gryphon pack, the hounds of Zeus,

162

As keen of fang as silent of their tongues!
Beware the one-eyed Arimaspian band
That tramp on horse-hoofs, dwelling by the ford
Of Pluto and the stream that flows with gold:
Keep thou aloof from these. To the world's end
Thou comest at the last, the dark-faced tribe
That dwell beside the sources of the sun,
Where springs the river, Aethiopian named.
Make thou thy way along his bank, until
Thou come unto the mighty downward slope
Where from the overland of Bybline hills
Nile pours his hallowed earth-refreshing wave.
He by his course shall guide thee to the realm
Named from himself, three-angled, water-girt;
There, Io, at the last, hath Fate ordained,
For thee and for thy race, the charge to found,
Far from thy native shore, a new abode.
Lo, I have said: if aught hereof appear
Hard to thy sense and inarticulate,
Question me o'er again, and soothly learn—
God wot, I have too much of leisure here!

CHORUS

If there be aught beyond, or aught pass'd o'er,
Which thou canst utter, of her woe-worn maze,
Speak on! if all is said, then grant to us
That which we asked, as thou rememberest.

PROMETHEUS

She now hath learned, unto its utmost end,
Her pilgrimage; but yet, that she may know
That 'tis no futile fable she hath heard,
I will recount her history of toil
Ere she came hither; let it stand for proof
Of what I told, my forecast of the end.
So, then—to sum in brief the weary tale—
I turn me to thine earlier exile's close.
When to Molossia's lowland thou hadst come,
Nigh to Dodona's cliff and ridge sublime,
(Where is the shrine oracular and seat
Of Zeus, Thesprotian styled, and that strange thing

And marvel past belief, the prophet-oaks
That syllable his speech), thou by their tongues,
With clear acclaim and unequivocal,
Wert thus saluted — *Hail, O bride of Zeus*
That art to be — hast memory thereof?
Thence, stung anew with frenzy, thou didst hie
Along the shoreward track, to Rhea's lap,
The mighty main; then, stormily distraught,
Backward again and eastward. To all time,
Be well assured, that inlet of the sea
All mortal men shall call Ionian,
In memory that Io fared thereby.
Take this for proof and witness that my mind
Hath more in ken than ever sense hath shown.
(*To the* CHORUS)
That which remains, to you and her alike
I will relate, and, to my former words
Reverting, add this final prophecy.
(*To* Io)
There lieth, at the verge of land and sea,
Where Nilus issues thro' the silted sand,
A town, Canopus called: and there at length
Shall Zeus renew the reason in thy brain
With the mere touch and contact of his hand
Fraught now with fear no more: and thou shalt bear
A child, dark Epaphus — his very name
Memorial of Zeus' touch that gave him life.
And his shall be the foison and the fruit
Of all the land enriched by spreading Nile.
Thence the fifth generation of his seed
Back unto Argos, yet unwillingly,
Shall flee for refuge — fifty maidens they,
Loathing a wedlock with their next in blood,
More kin than kind, from their sire's brother sprung.
And on their track, astir with wild desire,
Like falcons fierce closing on doves that flee,
Shall speed the suitors, craving to achieve
A prey forbidden, a reluctant bride.
Yet power divine shall foil them, and forbid
Possession of the maids, whom Argive land
Shall hold protected, when unsleeping hate,
Horror, and watchful ambush of the night,
Have laid the suitors dead, by female hands.

For every maid shall smite a man to death,
Dyeing a dagger's edges in his throat—
Such bed of love befall mine enemies!
Yet in one bride shall yearning conquer hate,
Bidding her spare the bridegroom at her side,
Blunting the keen edge of her set resolve.
Thus of two scorns the former shall she choose,
The name of coward, not of murderess.
In Argos shall she bear, in after time,
A royal offspring. Long it were to tell
In clear succession all that thence shall be.
Take this for sooth—in lineage from her
A hero shall arise, an archer great,
And he shall be my saviour from these woes.
Such knowledge of the future Themis gave,
The ancient Titaness, to me her son.
But how, and by what skill, 'twere long to say,
And no whit will the knowledge profit thee.

IO

O woe, O rending and convulsive pain,
Frenzy and agony, again, again
Searing my heart and brain!
O dagger of the sting, unforged with fire
Yet burning, burning ever! O my heart,
Pulsing with horror, beating at my breast!
O rolling maddened eyes! away, apart,
Raving with anguish dire,
I spring, by frenzy-fiends possest.
O wild and whirling words, that sweep in gloom
Down to dark waves of doom!
[*Exit* IO.

CHORUS

O well and sagely was it said—
Yea, wise of heart was he who first
Gave forth in speech the thought he nursed—
In thine own order see thou wed!

Let not the humble heart aspire
To the gross home of wealth and pride;

165

Nor be it to a hearth allied
That vaunts of many a noble sire.

O Fates, of awful empery!
Never may I by Zeus be wooed—
Never give o'er my maidenhood
To any god that dwells on high.

A shudder to my soul is sent,
Beholding Io's doom forlorn—
By Hera's malice put to scorn,
Roaming in mateless banishment.

From wedlock's crown of fair desire
I would not shrink—an idle fear!
But may no god to me draw near
With shunless might and glance of fire!

That were a strife wherein no chance
Of conquest lies: from Zeus most high
And his resolve, no subtlety
Could win me my deliverance.

PROMETHEUS

And yet shall Zeus, for all his stubborn pride,
Be brought to low estate! aha, he schemes
Such wedlock as shall bring his doom on him,
Flung from his kingship to oblivion's lap!
Ay, then the curse his father Cronos spake
As he fell helpless from his agelong throne,
Shall be fulfilled unto the utterance!
No god but I can manifest to him
A rescue from such ruin as impends—
I know it, I, and how it may be foiled.
Go to, then, let him sit and blindly trust
His skyey rumblings, for security,
And wave his levin with its blast of flame!
All will avail him not, nor bar his fall
Down to dishonour vile, intolerable
So strong a wrestler is he moulding now
To his own proper downfall—yea, a shape
Portentous and unconquerably huge,

166

Who truly shall reveal a flame more strong
Than is the lightning, and a crash of sound
More loud than thunder, and shall dash to nought
Poseidon's trident-spear, the ocean-bane
That makes the firm earth quiver. Let Zeus strike
Once on this rock, he speedily shall learn
How far the fall from power to slavery!

CHORUS

Beware! thy wish doth challenge Zeus himself.

PROMETHEUS

I voice my wish and its fulfilment too.

CHORUS

What, dare we look for one to conquer Zeus?

PROMETHEUS

Ay—Zeus shall wear more painful bonds than mine

CHORUS

Darest thou speak such taunts and tremble not?

PROMETHEUS

Why should I fear, who am immortal too?

CHORUS

Yet he might doom thee to worse agony.

PROMETHEUS

Out on his dooming! I foreknow it all.

CHORUS

Yet do the wise revere Necessity.

PROMETHEUS

Ay, ay—do reverence, cringe and crouch to power
Whene'er, where'er thou see it! But, for me,
I reck of Zeus as something less than nought.
Let him put forth his power, attest his sway,
Howe'er he will—a momentary show,
A little brief authority in heaven!
Aha, I see out yonder one who comes,
A bidden courier, truckling at Zeus' nod,
A lacquey in his new lord's livery,
Surely on some fantastic errand sped!
[*Enter* HERMES.
HERMES

Thou, double-dyed in gall of bitterness,
Trickster and sinner against gods, by giving
The stolen fire to perishable men!
Attend—the Sire supreme doth bid thee tell
What is the wedlock which thou vauntest now,
Whereby he falleth from supremacy?
Speak forth the whole, make all thine utterance clear,
Have done with words inscrutable, nor cause
To me, Prometheus! any further toil
Or twofold journeying. Go to—thou seest
Zeus doth not soften at such words as thine!

PROMETHEUS

Pompous, in sooth, thy word, and swoln with pride,
As doth befit the lacquey of thy lords!
O ye young gods! how, in your youthful sway,
Ye deem secure your citadels of sky,
Beyond the reach of sorrow or of fall!
Have I not seen two dynasties of gods
Already flung therefrom? and soon shall see
A third, that now in tyranny exults,
Shamed, ruined, in an hour! What sayest thou?
Crouch I and tremble at these stripling powers?
Small homage unto such from me, or none!
Betake thee hence, sweat back along thy road—
Look for no answer from me, get thee gone!

HERMES

Think—it was such audacities of will
That drove thee erst to anchorage in woe!

PROMETHEUS

Ay—but mark this: mine heritage of pain
I would not barter for thy servitude.

HERMES

Better, forsooth, be bond-slave to a crag,
Than true-born herald unto Zeus the Sire!

PROMETHEUS

Take thine own coin—taunts for a taunting slave!

HERMES

Proud art thou in thy circumstance, methinks!

PROMETHEUS

Proud? in such pride then be my foemen set,
And I to see—and of such foes art thou!

HERMES

What, blam'st thou me too for thy sufferings?

PROMETHEUS

Mark a plain word—I loathe all gods that are,
Who reaped my kindness and repay with wrong.

HERMES

I hear no little madness in thy words.

PROMETHEUS

Madness be mine, if scorn of foes be mad.

HERMES

Past bearing were thy pride, in happiness.

PROMETHEUS

Ah me!

HERMES

Zeus knoweth nought of sorrow's cry!

PROMETHEUS

He shall! Time's lapse bringeth all lessons home.

HERMES

To thee it brings not yet discretion's curb.

PROMETHEUS

No—else I had not wrangled with a slave!

HERMES

Then thou concealest all that Zeus would learn?

PROMETHEUS

As though I owed him aught and should repay!

HERMES

Scornful thy word, as though I were a child—

PROMETHEUS

Child, ay—or whatsoe'er hath less of brain—
Thou, deeming thou canst wring my secret out!
No mangling torture, no, nor sleight of power
There is, by which he shall compel my speech,
Until these shaming bonds be loosed from me.
So, let him fling his blazing levin-bolt!
Let him with white and winged flakes of snow,
And rumbling earthquakes, whelm and shake the world!
For nought of this shall bend me to reveal
The power ordained to hurl him from his throne.

HERMES

Bethink thee if such words can mend thy lot

PROMETHEUS

All have I long foreseen, and all resolved.

HERMES

Perverse of will! constrain, constrain thy soul
To think more wisely in the grasp of doom!

PROMETHEUS

Truce to vain words! as wisely wouldst thou strive
To warn a swelling wave: imagine not
That ever I before thy lord's resolve
Will shrink in womanish terror, and entreat,
As with soft suppliance of female hands,
The Power I scorn unto the utterance,
To loose me from the chains that bind me here—
A world's division 'twixt that thought and me!

HERMES

So, I shall speak, whate'er I speak, in vain!
No prayer can melt or soften thy resolve;
But, as a colt new-harnessed champs the bit,
Thou strivest and art restive to the rein.
But all too feeble is the stratagem
In which thou art so confident: for know
That strong self-will is weak and less than nought
In one more proud than wise. Bethink thee now —
If these my words thou shouldest disregard —
What storm, what might as of a great third wave
Shall dash thy doom upon thee, past escape!
First shall the Sire, with thunder and the flame
Of lightning, rend the crags of this ravine,
And in the shattered mass o'erwhelm thy form,
Immured and morticed in a clasping rock.
Thence, after age on age of durance done,
Back to the daylight shall thou come, and there
The eagle-hound of Zeus, red-ravening, fell
With greed, shall tatter piecemeal all thy flesh
To shreds and ragged vestiges of form —
Yea, an unbidden guest, a day-long bane,
That feeds, and feeds — yea, he shall gorge his fill
On blackened fragments, from thy vitals gnawed.
Look for no respite from that agony
Until some other deity be found,
Ready to bear for thee the brunt of doom,
Choosing to pass into the lampless world
Of Hades and the murky depths of hell.
Hereat, advise thee! 'tis no feigned threat
Whereof I warn thee, but an o'er-true tale.
The lips of Zeus know nought of lying speech,
But wreak in action all their words foretell.
Therefore do thou look warily, and deem
Prudence a better saviour than self-will.

CHORUS

Meseems that Hermes speaketh not amiss,
Bidding thee leave thy wilfulness and seek
The wary walking of a counselled mind.
Give heed! to err through anger shames the wise.

PROMETHEUS

All, all I knew, whate'er his tongue
In idle arrogance hath flung.
'Tis the world's way, the common lot—
Foe tortures foe and pities not.
Therefore I challenge him to dash
His bolt on me, his zigzag flash
Of piercing, rending flame!
Now be the welkin stirred amain
With thunder-peal and hurricane,
And let the wild winds now displace
From its firm poise and rooted base
The stubborn earthly frame!
The raging sea with stormy surge
Rise up and ravin and submerge
Each high star-trodden way!
Me let him lift and dash to gloom
Of nether hell, in whirls of doom!
Yet—do he what extremes he may—
He cannot crush my life away!

HERMES

Such are the counsels, such the strain,
Heard from wild lips and frenzied brain!
In word or thought, how fails his fate
Of madness wild and desperate?
(*To the* CHORUS)
But ye, who stand compassionate
Here at his side, depart in haste!
Lest of his penalty ye taste,
And shattered brain and reason feel
The roaring, ruthless thunder-peal!

CHORUS

Out on thee! if thy heart be fain
I should obey thee, change thy strain!
Vile is thine hinted cowardice,
And loathed of me thy base advice,
Weakly to shrink from pain!
Nay, at his side, whate'er befall,
I will abide, endure it all!
Among all things abhorr'd, accurst,
I hold betrayers for the worst!

HERMES

Nay, ye are warned! remember well—
Nor cry, when meshed in nets of hell,
Ah cruel fate, ah Zeus unkind—
Thus, by a sentence undivined,
To dash us to the realms below!
It is no sudden, secret blow—
Nay, ye achieve your proper woe—
Warn'd and foreknowing shall ye go,
Through your own folly trapped and ta'en,
Into the net the Fates ordain—
The vast, illimitable pain!
[*Thunder and lightning.*

PROMETHEUS

Hark! for no more in empty word,
But in sheer sooth, the world is stirred!
The massy earth doth heave and sway,
And thro' their dark and secret way
The cavern'd thunders boom!
See, how they gleam athwart the sky,
The lightnings, through the gloom!
And whirlwinds roll the dust on high,
And right and left the storm-clouds leap
To battle in the skyey deep,
In wildest uproar unconfined,
An universe of warring wind!
And falling sky and heaving sea
Are blent in one! on me, on me,

Nearer and ever yet more near,
Flaunting its pageantry of fear,
Drives down in might its destined road
The tempest of the wrath of God!
O holy Earth, O mother mine!
O Sky, that biddest speed along
Thy vault the common Light divine, —
Be witness of my wrong!
[*The rocks are rent with fire and earthquake,
and fall, burying* PROMETHEUS *in the ruins.*

Printed in the United Kingdom
by Lightning Source UK Ltd.
127860UK00002B/185/A